AMERICANS
THE *Spirit* OF A *Nation*

FREDERICK DOUGLASS

"Truth Is of No Color"

Michael A. Schuman

Enslow Publishers, Inc.
40 Industrial Road
Box 398
Berkeley Heights, NJ 07922
USA

http://www.enslow.com

Library of Congress Cataloging-in-Publication Data

Schuman, Michael.
    Frederick Douglass : "truth is of no color" / Michael A. Schuman.
       p. cm. — (Americans—the spirit of a nation)
    Includes bibliographical references and index.
       Summary: "Explores the life of Frederick Douglass, including his childhood in
slavery, his escape to freedom, and how he became one of the most famous
abolitionists, speakers, and writers in America"—Provided by publisher.
    ISBN-13: 978-0-7660-3025-1
    ISBN-10: 0-7660-3025-3
       1. Douglass, Frederick, 1818–1895—Juvenile literature. 2. African American
abolitionists—Biography—Juvenile literature. 3. Abolitionists—United States—
Biography—Juvenile literature. 4. Antislavery movements—United
States—History—19th century—Juvenile literature. I. Title.
    E449.D75S39 2009
    973.8'092—dc22
    [B]
                            2008029634

Printed in the United States of America

10 9 8 7 6 5 4 3 2 1

To Our Readers:
We have done our best to make sure all Internet Addresses in this book were active
and appropriate when we went to press. However, the author and the publisher have
no control over and assume no liability for the material available on those Internet
sites or on other Web sites they may link to. Any comments or suggestions can be sent
by e-mail to comments@enslow.com or to the address on the back cover.

♻ Enslow Publishers, Inc., is committed to printing our books on recycled paper. The
paper in every book contains 10% to 30% post-consumer waste (PCW). The cover
board on the outside of each book contains 100% PCW. Our goal is to do our part to
help young people and the environment too!

Illustration Credits: Courtesy of the Division of Special Collections, Archives, and
Rare Books, University of Missouri at Columbia, p. 34; Enslow Publishers, Inc., pp. 9,
87; The Granger Collection, New York, pp. 1, 4, 11, 16, 20, 24, 27, 36, 39, 67, 74,
81; Library of Congress, pp. 7, 18, 42, 50–51, 52, 56, 61, 68, 72–73, 83, 91, 92, 99,
100, 105, 110; Courtesy of Nancy Davis Kho, p. 111; National Archives and Records
Administration, p. 29; National Park Service, pp. 96, 108; National Portrait Gallery,
Smithsonian Institution / Art Resource, NY, p. 58; © North Wind / North Wind
Picture Archives, pp. 45, 54; Courtesy of Rocco Staino, p. 103.

Cover Illustration: The Granger Collection, New York (Portrait of Frederick
Douglass).

CONTENTS

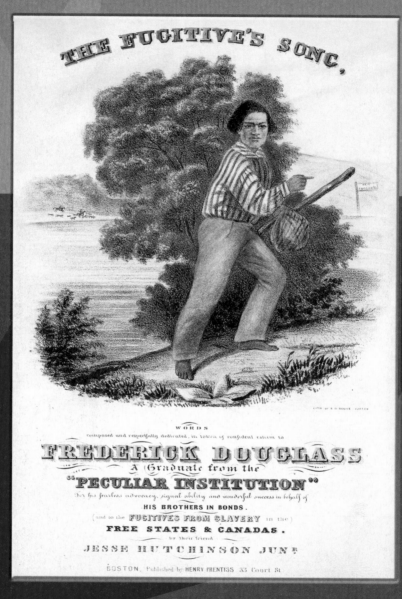

The cover of a song sheet for "The Fugitive's Song" depicts Frederick Douglass's escape from slavery. The song sheet was published in Boston in 1845.

Chapter

1

Escape!

On the morning of Monday, September 3, 1838, the man who would become Frederick Douglass put on a red shirt and tied a black scarf around his neck. As a finishing touch, he fitted a sailor's hat on top of his head. He then hopped inside a carriage driven by Isaac Rolls, an African-American friend. Rolls drove the carriage for a living, like a taxi driver would today. Their destination was the train station in Baltimore, Maryland.

Frederick was the slave to Thomas Auld of Maryland. Frederick was on one of the most dangerous journies of his life. He was escaping slavery. If Frederick were caught, his captors would return him to his owner. His owner might beat him as punishment.

Frederick carried a paper that identified him as a retired sailor. That gave him what was known as "seaman's protection." But the paper did not belong to Frederick. A black merchant sailor Frederick knew let him use it. The paper meant that he had served his country as a sailor and was entitled to the same rights as any retired serviceman.

Frederick could not simply walk to the ticket window and buy a ticket like a regular passenger. The ticket seller would closely examine the paper. It would be clear that the paper was not Frederick's. Instead, Frederick and Rolls sat and waited for the next train heading north to start up its engines.

Just as it did, Frederick took his luggage, ran, and jumped aboard. Nobody asked to look at his documents until the train was about forty miles northeast of Baltimore. Frederick later wrote that his heart pounded faster than a deer or fox being chased by hungry dogs.

The conductor sternly checked the papers of other African-American passengers in the railcar. When the conductor approached Frederick, his mood changed. He acted friendly toward this man he thought to be a sailor. The conductor asked Frederick for his free papers. Frederick responded that he did not have his free papers, but something better. He pulled out the seaman's papers illustrated with a patriotic American eagle.

The conductor saw the eagle and gave Frederick a smile. He did not bother to look closely at the paper. He merely collected Frederick's train fare and let him be.

At the time of Frederick Douglass's escape, trains were just coming into regular use. This sketch from 1839 shows a train crossing Tiber Creek near Washington, D.C.

Frederick was not yet safe. He was still in Maryland. He wrote:

> *Though I was not a murderer fleeing from justice, I felt perhaps quite as miserable as such a criminal. The train was moving at a very high rate of speed for that epoch of railroad travel, but to my anxious mind it was moving far too slowly. Minutes were hours, and hours were days during this part of my flight.*[1]

Frederick saw several men, both black and white, that he recognized on the train.[2] Any of them may have seen him in his sailor's disguise and turned him in for a reward. The train's journey was over when the tracks ended at the Susquehanna River. Train passengers had to take a ferry across the waterway. They would board another train heading north after getting off the ferry.

On the ferry, Frederick heard someone call out to him. Frederick turned and recognized an acquaintance from Baltimore. He was an African-American man named Nichols who had no idea that Frederick was escaping slavery. He asked Frederick why he was on the train and why he wore that sailor's outfit. He then asked where Frederick was going, and when he planned on returning to Baltimore.

The last thing Frederick needed was Nichols asking questions. Anyone overhearing the conversation would realize Frederick was not who he pretended to be. Like a child playing hooky, Frederick answered as little as possible. When the chance arose, he ducked away from Nichols and went to another part of the boat.

After leaving the ferry, Frederick boarded a north-bound train for Delaware. While on board the train, Frederick saw another person he knew. He was a white blacksmith named Frederick Steen. They sat nearby in the same car. Frederick Douglass later wrote that Steen "looked at me very intently, as if he thought he had seen me somewhere before in his travels. I really believe he knew me, but had no heart to betray me. At any rate, he saw me escaping and held his peace."[3]

Frederick left the train in Wilmington, Delaware's biggest city. Wilmington was filled with bounty hunters who made money by capturing escaped slaves. According to government law, slaves were the property

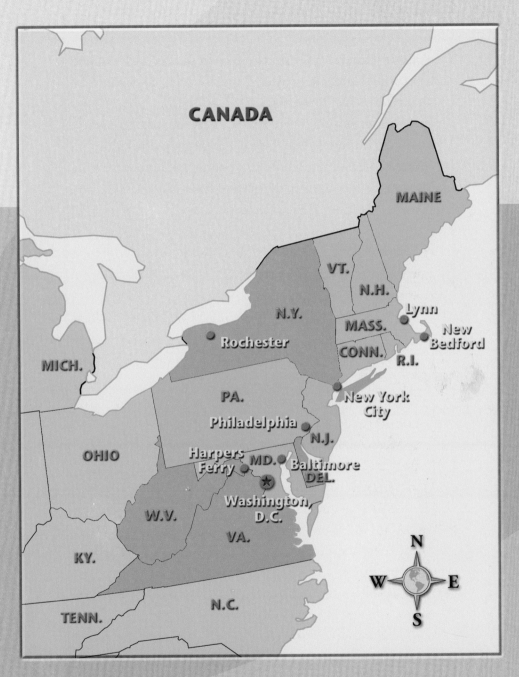

This map of the present-day United States shows the different places Frederick Douglass lived, along with other towns that were important in his life.

of their owners. So even though Frederick had escaped from Maryland, he belonged to his owner and could be returned to his home state.

No one bothered Frederick as he boarded a steamboat for Philadelphia. Upon arriving in Philadelphia Monday afternoon, Frederick spent a few hours catching his breath. He was finally on free soil.

When Reading Was a Crime

Frederick Douglass was born into slavery in February 1818. Since birth records were not kept for slaves, there is no way of knowing his exact birth date. For much of his life Douglass thought he was born in 1817.

Frederick's birthplace was Holmes Hill Farm, near the town of Easton, Maryland. His given name was Frederick Augustus Washington Bailey.

Slavery in the United States

Slavery in the New World was based on skin color. However, slavery in earlier times was not. The word slave comes from the word *Slavic*.[1] The Slavic people live in Eastern Europe and many have blond hair and blue eyes.

Africans were brought against their will as early as 1619 to Jamestown, Virginia. Jamestown was the first permanent settlement in what is now the United States. Some Africans in early America were indentured servants, which means they agreed to work for others for a period of time. When that time was up, indentured servants were usually given their own land and were allowed to work it for their own use and profit.

Other Africans were brought to the New World to work as slaves. By the late 1600s, slavery existed in all thirteen original colonies. By 1787, these colonies had become the United States.

Slavery was gradually abolished in the northern United States between the mid-1700s and the early 1800s. However, it was not banned in New York State until 1827.[2] When Douglass was born, slavery was legal and a way of life in the entire South and border states, including Maryland. Southern plantation and farm owners used slave labor to run their properties.

Historian and author William W. Gwaltney said of American slaves, "They could not control where they went, what they did, what they ate, who they could marry, or even how they would conduct their religious lives."[3] However, many married in secret, held church hidden in the woods, ran away, and sometimes rebelled. Douglass himself showed that owners could not always control slaves.

Frederick's mother was a slave named Harriet Bailey. His father is believed to be his first owner, Aaron Anthony.[4] Harriet worked long hours picking tobacco in the fields on a farm twelve miles away from Frederick. She had no time to take care of him. So he lived with his grandmother, Betsey Bailey. Betsey was too old to work in the fields. Her job was to take care of Harriet's children until they were old enough to work as slaves.

A Long Walk

Harriet could see her son rarely. She had to walk twelve miles after a long day in the tobacco fields. After visiting Frederick, she made the same long trip home. Frederick wrote: "I never saw my mother, to know her as such, more than four or five times in my life; and each of these times was very short in duration, and at night."[5] He added, "I do not recollect of ever seeing my mother by the light of day."[6]

Frederick's grandmother took on the traditional role of a mother. Historian Vincent Harding said, "His grandmother is someone who interprets the world for him and helps him to understand what he sees. Her faith in him, her confidence in him, her sense that he is meant to be something very important is a part of that necessary building of himself."[7]

Frederick spent his days as a young child splashing and playing in nearby Tuckahoe Creek. He also liked to imitate the noises made by the farm animals. His meals nearly always consisted of cornmeal mush. The only garments he and the other slave children wore were linen shirts that hung to their knees.

Home at the Wye House

When Frederick turned six, it was time for him to go to work. He and his grandmother walked about twelve miles to his new home. It was called Wye House and was located on a plantation owned by a man named Edward Lloyd. Even though Lloyd owned the plantation, Aaron Anthony managed it. As a manager, Anthony made sure operations on the plantation ran smoothly. That included making sure the slaves did what he demanded.

Frederick's siblings, Perry, Sara, and Eliza were already living and working there. Frederick had never met them before, and Betsey told Frederick to go join them. Betsey then returned home without saying good-bye. When Frederick saw Betsey had gone, he cried and cried. He realized he would be living with people he did not know. As a child, he had no choice but to do what these new people told him.

One morning, Frederick heard screams of pain coming from the Wye House kitchen. He peeked inside and saw Aaron Anthony whipping Frederick's Aunt Hester. Anthony was punishing her for being absent when he needed her to work. As he whipped Hester on her back, Anthony swore at her and called her disgusting names. She shrieked and cried, but Anthony did not stop. He whipped her so hard that blood oozed from her back and dripped onto the floor. As he continued whipping her, Anthony said, "I'll learn you how to disobey my orders!"[8]

Frederick was scared he would get caught watching. He wrote: "I was so terrified and horror-stricken at the sight, that I hid myself in a closet, and dared not venture out till long after the bloody transaction was over. I expected it would be my turn next. It was all new to me. I had never seen anything like it before."[9]

Some time early in 1825, Frederick's mother, Harriet, walked the long journey to visit him. She gave Frederick a present—a heart-shaped ginger cake. While at the Wye House, Harriet paid a visit to the cook, a slave the kids called Aunt Katy. Aunt Katy treated Frederick like a stray dog. She purposely let him go hungry. Harriet scolded Aunt Katy and told her to take better care of her son.

Not long afterward, Harriet Bailey died. Historians believe it was either in late 1825 or early in 1826. Frederick did not find out until some time later. Since Frederick had hardly gotten to know her, he said he felt "no strong emotions of sorrow for her."[10] He said that it was many years after her death that he appreciated her value as his mother.

Another Move

When Frederick was eight, he was sent to Baltimore to live with a married couple, Hugh and Sophia Auld. The Aulds had a two-year-old son named Thomas. Hugh Auld's brother, also named Thomas, was married to Aaron Anthony's daughter, Lucretia.

Harriet Bailey protected Frederick from Aunt Katy, who was mistreating him. This illustration appeared in one of Frederick Douglass's autobiographies, The Life and Times of Frederick Douglass, *published in 1881.*

Life with the Aulds was much different than at the Wye House. The Wye House was in the Maryland countryside. Frederick's new home was in an exciting and busy port city. Frederick said good-bye to farm life and learned a new trade—helping Hugh Auld in his shipbuilding business.

The Aulds were kinder than Aaron Anthony and Aunt Katy. They treated Frederick more like a stepson than a slave. He wore pants and shirts, instead of just long linen shirts. His owners fed him bread rather than cornmeal mush. Sophia Auld liked to read Bible stories to both the younger Thomas and Frederick.

Frederick started to feel at home with the Auld family. But then in November 1826, he received shocking news. Aaron Anthony had died. He did not leave a will. A will is a legal document declaring who gets one's money and property after his or her death.

Anthony's property was divided among his children. Eight-year-old Frederick was ordered to go back to the Wye House. On a late fall morning in 1827, Frederick boarded a boat taking him across Chesapeake Bay to Tuckahoe Creek. Frederick hated to leave, and the Aulds were sorry to see him go. "We, all three, wept bitterly," Frederick later recalled.[11]

A Brief Reunion

Soon after he arrived, he saw his grandmother Betsey for the first time in nearly a year. Frederick, Betsey, and the other members of the Bailey family were lined up in a row. Anthony's family members were about to pick

In 1831, W. J. Bennett painted this view of Baltimore from across the harbor showing ships and wharves with the city in the background. Baltimore was Frederick's first experience with city life.

who they wanted to be their slaves. Luckily for Frederick, Hugh Auld grabbed the rights to both Frederick and his sister, Eliza.

The Aulds had really taken a liking to the youngster. Frederick lived with them in Baltimore for more than five years. He never saw most of his blood relatives again. But the Aulds became a kind of new family. He saw little of the older Thomas Auld. Thomas Auld had remarried and moved to another town, St. Michaels, Maryland.

Frederick worked as an errand boy and general assistant at Hugh Auld's shipyard. Sometimes, shipyard workers wrote letters on lumber. The letters indicated where the wood should be placed on a boat. For example, they might write the letter L for left and R for right. Frederick would often copy the letters to familiarize himself with them. He had never been taught the alphabet.

Learning to Read

When Frederick was not at work, Sophia continued to read the Bible to him and her son, Thomas. As he watched her read, Frederick was fascinated with the idea of letters on a page forming words. He finally mustered the courage to ask Sophia to teach him to read. At first, she was happy to do so, despite the fact that teaching a slave to read was illegal in Maryland.

Sophia helped Frederick form a few words and was very proud of her accomplishments. One day she showed her husband how Frederick could read.

Sophia had not expected her husband's reaction. The idea of a slave being able to read angered Hugh. Hugh may have treated Frederick as a son, but Frederick was still a slave. Hugh said to Sophia, "If you learn him how to read, he'll want to know how to write; and this accomplished, he'll be running away with himself."[12] On Hugh's insistence, Sophia stopped teaching Frederick to read.

Young Teachers in the Neighborhood

However, it was too late for the Aulds; Frederick had caught the reading bug. Since he could no longer rely on

At first, Sophia Auld taught Frederick how to read.

Sophia Auld to help him learn, Frederick found some new teachers—white boys he hung around with in his neighborhood. Even though there was plenty of racism in the United States, Frederick said the white boys he knew were very sympathetic toward him. He admitted, "I do not remember ever to have met with a boy, while I was in slavery, who defended the slave system; but I have often had boys to console me, with the hope that something would yet occur, by which I might be made free."[13]

Sometimes he encountered these boys while running errands for the Aulds. Other times he asked them to help him practice reading while playing with them. Frederick had no money, so he paid them with pieces of bread instead. Many of these boys were poor and hungry, so they were happy to teach Frederick for food. Frederick later wrote, "The plan which I mainly adopted, and the one which was most successful, was that of using my young white playmates, with whom I met on the streets, as teachers."[14] Frederick had reading contests with his white friends. The contests showed who had better reading skills. It did not matter if he won the contests because he would learn to read better by watching the other boys compete.

Historian Lerone Bennett said, "Douglass from that point on was in love with words, in love with reading. He hid books in his pocket, pieces of paper in his pocket, and he read everything he possibly could read."[15]

One book he often carried was *The American Spelling Book*, written by Noah Webster. Webster is best known today for writing the first American dictionary. But he also wrote a speller in the early 1800s. Teachers used the speller to help children pronounce and spell simple words.

Sneaking Around

In addition to the speller, Frederick kept a Methodist hymnal and Bible with him. He also borrowed books that the Aulds' son, Thomas, had outgrown. Frederick had to be careful not to be caught reading and writing. He often snuck behind warehouses to practice on his own.

After a few years, Frederick was able to read newspapers and government documents. Through reading these papers, he first learned about the abolitionist movement.

He read that congressmen were introducing bills to stop the spread of slavery. Frederick later said, "From that moment, I understood the direct pathway from slavery to freedom."[16]

When Frederick was about thirteen, he earned a little money shining men's boots. He then went to a neighborhood bookstore and plunked down fifty cents to buy a special book. (That is equal to about nine dollars today.[17]) It was titled *The Columbian Orator*.

The Columbian Orator

The pages of *The Columbian Orator* were filled with poems, political essays, speeches, and classic writings dating from ancient Rome to Frederick's time. All had one thing in common; they promoted patriotism and good values. Teachers used *The Columbian Orator* in classrooms in the early 1800s. A Connecticut-born author named Caleb Bingham had edited the book.

The Columbian Orator frontispiece, or page before the title page, read in part that its purpose was "calculated to improve youth and others in the ornamental and useful art of eloquence."[18] *The Columbian Orator* can still be found online and in print today.

The selection from *The Columbian Orator* that most intrigued Frederick was a short play titled *Slave in Barbary*. It takes place in the 1700s. At the play's end, a slave owner frees one of the slaves he planned to sell.

Another piece in *The Columbian Orator* was titled "Dialogue between Master and Slave." In it the master, or owner, tells the slave that he has been a kind owner. He then says the slave should be grateful that a softhearted man owns him. The slave responds that kindness is good, but nothing makes up for freedom. So the owner frees the slave. The owner expects to be thanked. Instead, the ex-slave warns his former owner that slaves are angry—and they have a right to be. Some day they may try to exact revenge against their owners.

That passage left a huge impression on Frederick. It made him think that some day he might be able to talk back to his owner the way the slave did in "Dialogue between Master and Slave." Frederick also began to think about taking a bold step—running away.

Chapter

3

Breaking the
Slave Breaker

When Frederick was fifteen, he was sent to yet another home to live. The location of his new home was St. Michaels, Maryland. The owner was Hugh Auld's brother, Thomas, and his new wife, Rowena.

At first, Thomas Auld and Frederick were happy to see each other. Even though he was a slave, Frederick had always gotten some respect from the Auld family. However, Frederick soon learned that

Rowena Auld was not as kind to her slaves as Hugh and Sophia had been.

All the years of reading the Bible had made Frederick a Christian believer. Frederick did not understand how Thomas Auld or any other Christian could own slaves. In August 1833, he convinced Auld to attend a religious rally in St. Michaels. Frederick thought Auld could be inspired to understand the evil of slavery.

Frederick Douglass later wrote: "'If he has got religion,' thought I, 'he will emancipate his slaves; and if he should not do so much as this, he will, at any rate, behave toward us more kindly, and feed us more generously than he has heretofore done.'"[1] The idea of Christians defending slavery outraged Frederick.[2]

But the only minister who spoke out against slavery was named George Cookman. One slave owner took Cookman's words to heart and freed his slaves. No one else did. There was no change in Auld's relationship with his slaves. Douglass wrote: "But in my expectations I was double disappointed. Master Thomas was *Master Thomas* still.[3]

Rebelling Against Mr. Auld

Frederick then rebelled against Auld in subtle ways. He performed his tasks poorly. He purposely forgot orders or lost tools. Rowena Auld responded by withholding meals. She thought if the slaves were hungry, they would work harder.

That action had an opposite effect. Frederick stole food. He knew it was morally wrong to steal, but he also knew slavery was morally wrong.[4] Of the two actions, Frederick felt slavery was more immoral.

Since the Aulds found Frederick difficult, Thomas Auld hired him out to a farmer living nearby, Edward Covey. Covey was known for his skill in "breaking" slaves. "Breaking" meant taking slaves that were thought to be difficult and turning them into productive laborers. A slave breaker usually tried to get slaves to work by whipping or beating them.

Three Thousand Pounds of Oxen and Frederick

In early January 1834, Frederick, now sixteen, arrived at the Covey farm. Almost as soon as he did, Covey sent him out on a job completely new to him. He demanded that Frederick take a pair of oxen and a cart into the woods two miles away. There he was to gather a bundle of fresh-cut lumber and bring it back to the farm. Frederick had worked mostly in the city of Baltimore and had done little farmwork. Having no experience with oxen, Frederick did not know what to do.

Covey gave Frederick brief instructions. He tied a ten-foot rope around the oxen's horns and handed the rope to Frederick to control them. Those few instructions were not enough to acquaint Frederick with the tricky job of working with oxen. Shortly after he took the oxen into the woods, they bolted. Two oxen weighing about fifteen hundred pounds each barreled through the woods. Frederick, who weighed less than two hundred pounds, gave chase.

The oxen smashed a gate, crashed through fences, and banged from side to side against trees. At one point, Frederick got in their way and had to jump aside. Finally, the oxen came to a halt amid a deep thicket of woods.

The animals were stuck and they had severely damaged the cart. Frederick untangled the oxen from the thicket and tried leading them home. On his way, he stopped to open a gate. Before he had time to grab the rope to lead the oxen through the open gate, the animals took off again. They were out of control and smashed the cart to pieces.

Two oxen were a lot for Frederick to handle, especially since he had never dealt with such beasts before.

The Cruel Mr. Covey

When he returned to Covey's farm, Frederick explained how he lost control of the oxen because of his lack of experience. Covey had no sympathy for Frederick. He marched Frederick into the woods, took out a jackknife, and cut three switches from a gum tree. He then ordered Frederick to strip naked. Frederick refused, but Covey repeated his order. Frederick refused again. Finally, Covey tore off Frederick's shirt and whipped him on his back. From then on, Frederick was whipped by Covey on a regular basis.[5]

Frederick could take only so much. On a hot August day in 1834, he was harvesting wheat with a few other slaves. His labor in the torrid summer sun gave him heatstroke, in which the body cannot cope with the stress of the heat. Frederick had a brutal headache and felt dizzy. He crawled to a shady spot to catch his breath.

When Covey discovered Frederick, he kicked him and ordered him to get up. Frederick tried but could not get up. Covey kicked Frederick again and hit his head with a hunk of hickory wood. Blood gushed from the wound.

Frederick decided he had put up with enough brutality. After the heatstroke had subsided, he got up. When he was certain Covey was not watching, Frederick ran away. He could hear Covey call for him to come back. As Frederick looked back, he saw Covey saddling up a horse about to give chase. Frederick dashed into the woods to avoid Covey.

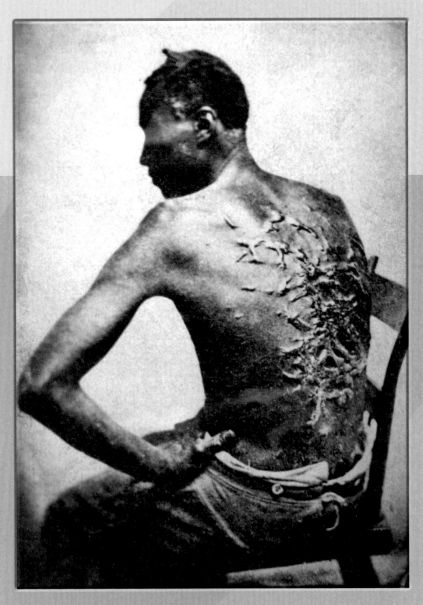

*After the incident with the oxen, Edward Covey whipped
Frederick nearly everyday. The scars on this slave's back
show the effects such violence can have. This picture was
taken after the slave had escaped slavery.*

A Daring Trek

Frederick's destination was the home of Thomas Auld, seven miles away. He planned to tell Auld how brutally Covey treated him. He hoped Auld would be sympathetic. If not, then perhaps he could make Auld angry by telling him how Covey treated his slave. Frederick walked barefoot seven miles through tangled woods and briars and brush. With his face bleeding and his clothes shredded, he reached the home of Thomas Auld.

When he found Auld, Frederick said, "Find me a new master."[6] Frederick told Auld that if he went back, Covey might kill him. Auld allowed Frederick to stay overnight on his property. But Auld said that in the morning Frederick must return to Covey.

While walking back to Covey's farm, Frederick ran into an African-American man named Sandy Jenkins. Some historians say he was a free man. Others say he was a slave married to a free African-American woman.

Jenkins and his wife gave Frederick shelter for the night, even though this act was against the law. Frederick finally arrived at Covey's farm the next morning, a Sunday. Frederick expected a savage beating. But the Covey family went into their horse-drawn wagon and drove to church. Covey considered himself a Christian, and to him the Sabbath was not an appropriate day to beat a slave.

Monday was different. Before dawn, Frederick stepped inside a barn to take care of the horses. He was halfway inside a hayloft, when Covey walked into the barn. Grabbing Frederick from behind, Covey threw

Frederick to the floor. He tried to tie Frederick's ankles with a rope, but Frederick slipped away.

Frederick wrote: "Mr. Covey seemed now to think he had me, and could do what he pleased; but at this moment—from whence came the spirit I don't know—I resolved to fight; and, suiting my action to the resolution, I seized Covey hard by the throat; and as I did so, I rose."[7]

A Bruising Fight

Covey and Frederick got into a brutal fight. As Covey continued to try to tie Frederick's hands, Covey called his cousin Bill Hughes over to help him. Frederick responded by kicking Hughes beneath the ribs. Hughes staggered away, and Covey realized he was dealing with a determined fighter.

Covey then called over a slave named Bill Smith to try to subdue Frederick. But Smith refused to do so. He said he had to do his job instead. A hardy female slave named Caroline walked by on her way to milk cows. Covey asked her to help him gain control of Frederick. Caroline was strong enough and Frederick was tired enough that she could have helped subdue him. Like Bill Smith, however, she refused. Covey had to fight Frederick on his own.

Frederick wrote: "I told him . . . that he had used me like a brute for six months, and that I was determined to be used so no longer."[8]

The fight lasted about two hours. Finally, Covey let Frederick go. Frederick wrote: "This battle with

Mr. Covey was the turning-point in my career as a slave. It rekindled the few expiring embers of freedom, and revived within me a sense of my own manhood. It recalled the departed self-confidence, and inspired me again with a determination to be free."[9]

The fight was a victory for Frederick in another way. From that point on, Covey stopped beating him. He hardly bothered Frederick again. Historians have tried to guess why. Covey could have easily ganged up on Frederick with family members or other local slave owners. Frederick said that Covey was embarrassed to admit that a sixteen-year-old slave had fought him to a standstill. If word got out, then Covey's reputation as a tough slave breaker would be ruined. Some Douglass historians think that Thomas Auld told Covey to no longer beat Frederick. Auld would not want his slave injured to the point that he could no longer work.

To the Freeland Farm

Frederick stayed with Covey until Christmas Day, 1834. He spent the holiday with the Aulds. Then in January he was hired out to another neighboring farmer, William Freeland. Freeland was kinder than Covey. Frederick was happy to see that Freeland was not a religious man and attended no church. Frederick had observed that "of all slaveholders . . . religious ones are the worst. I have found them, almost invariably, the vilest, meanest and basest of their class."[10]

Frederick showed his wit when he wrote: "But, by this time, I began to want to live *upon* free land as well as *with Freeland*; and I was no longer content, therefore, to live with him or any other slaveholder."[11]

A Secret School

Frederick started teaching slaves on the Freeland farm to read. He knew that was the surest thing to stir up slaves. But he also knew it was dangerous. If he was caught, he would likely be whipped or beaten. He found old shade trees or other hidden spots on the farm to conduct his secret reading classes.

Two of his best pupils were brothers named John and Henry Harris. In time, Frederick had as many as thirty slaves and free African-American men as students. Frederick used his favorite texts, *The Columbian Orator* and *Webster's Speller* as his teaching tools.

Later on, a free African-American man in the area let them use his house as a school. Even when Frederick wrote about the illegal school some twenty years later, he refused to name the home owner. That was too much of a risk.

The essays about freedom and slavery in *The Columbian Orator* put rebellious ideas in the minds of Frederick's students. While Frederick had thought about escaping for a while, now the time seemed right. He hatched a plan with the Harris brothers. Two other slaves from nearby farms, Charles Roberts and Henry Bailey, also joined the plot.

The last plot member was Sandy Jenkins, the African-American man who had sheltered Frederick on his way back to Covey's farm. The six men decided to

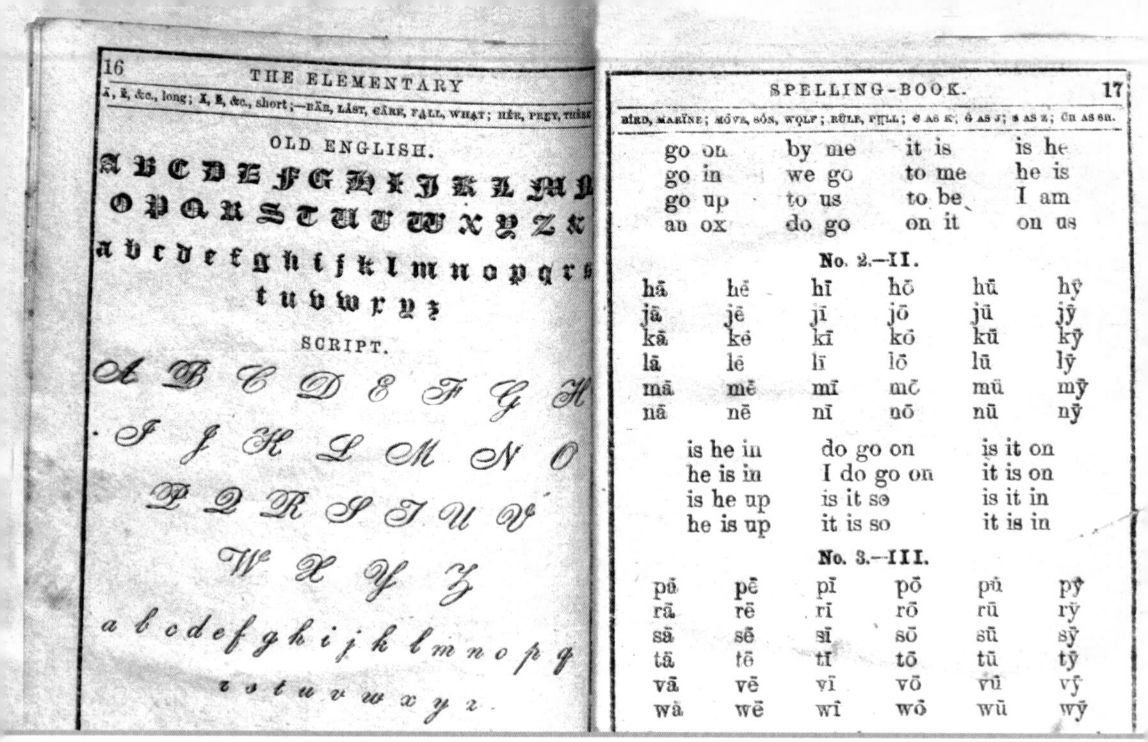
16 THE ELEMENTARY

Ā, Ē, &c., long; Ă, Ĕ, &c., short;—BÄR, LÅST, CÂRE, FALL, WHAT; HÊR, PREY, THÊRE

OLD ENGLISH.

A B C D E F G H I J K L M N
O P Q R S T U V W X Y Z &
a b c d e f g h i j k l m n o p q r s
t u v w x y z

SCRIPT.

A B C D E F G H
I J K L M N O
P Q R S T U V
W X Y Z
a b c d e f g h i j k l m n o p q
r s t u v w x y z

SPELLING-BOOK. 17

BÏRD, MARÏNE; MÓVE, SÓN, WOLF; RÛLE, PULL; € AS K; Ġ AS J; S AS Z; CH AS SH.

go on	by me	it is	is he
go in	we go	to me	he is
go up	to us	to be	I am
an ox	do go	on it	on us

No. 2.—II.

hā	hē	hī	hō	hū	hȳ
jā	jē	jī	jō	jū	jȳ
kā	kē	kī	kō	kū	kȳ
lā	lē	lī	lō	lū	lȳ
mā	mē	mī	mō	mū	mȳ
nā	nē	nī	nō	nū	nȳ

is he in	do go on	is it on
he is in	I do go on	it is on
is he up	is it so	is it in
he is up	it is so	it is in

No. 3.—III.

pā	pē	pī	pō	pū	pȳ
rā	rē	rī	rō	rū	rȳ
sā	sē	sī	sō	sū	sȳ
tā	tē	tī	tō	tū	tȳ
vā	vē	vī	vō	vū	vȳ
wā	wē	wī	wō	wū	wȳ

Frederick used books like* The Elementary Spelling Book *to teach other African Americans how to read and spell.

steal a canoe and sail north into free Pennsylvania. Upon reaching Pennsylvania, they would leave the canoe and escape on foot.

Just days before they were about to leave, Jenkins dropped out of the plot. He said he had a dream that predicted that Frederick would be captured. Frederick paid little attention to Jenkins's dream. He went ahead with his little group's escape plans on the night of Saturday, April 2, 1836.

Caught

The men went to work as usual Saturday morning. While Frederick and Jenkins were spreading manure in the fields, Frederick said he had a feeling that someone had told the authorities about their plot. Jenkins answered that he felt the same. As they headed to the house for breakfast, six men approached Frederick. Four were white men on horseback. The other two were black men walking behind with their hands tied.

Frederick recognized the black men as Charles Roberts and Henry Bailey, two of his fellow plotters. One of the white men on horseback was William Hambleton, Rowena Auld's father. The other three were members of the local law authority. They grabbed Frederick, tied him up, and took him into the Freeland kitchen.

Someone had told authorities about the escape plot. The five men were tied behind two horses and dragged three miles to St. Michaels. There they faced Frederick's owner, Thomas Auld. Auld demanded that they admit they were plotting to run away. The five men denied the charge. They said they never had plans to escape. It did not matter. The plotters were taken to the county jail in the city of Easton.

Frederick's biggest concern was that he would be sold to slave traders from the Deep South. He wrote: "The ever dreaded slave life in Georgia, Louisiana and Alabama—from which escape is next to impossible—now, in my loneliness, stared me in the face."[12] A group of slave traders were indeed allowed to enter the jail. They gave the five men personal and embarrassing examinations. They poked them in the stomach, felt their arms, and shook them by the shoulders to see how healthy they were. Frederick did not know what his fate would be. He also had one lingering question—who had betrayed them?

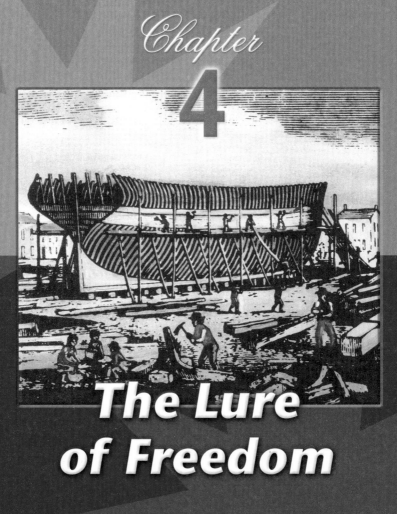

The Lure of Freedom

rederick came to one conclusion about the failed escape plot. He wrote: "Master Thomas would not tell us who his informant was, but we suspected, and suspected one person only. Several circumstances seemed to point Sandy out as our betrayer."[1] After all, Sandy Jenkins knew about the escape plans, then pulled out of the plot.

Yet Frederick did not want to believe it. He wrote of Jenkins: "We all loved him too well to think it possible that he could have betrayed us."[2]

For the rest of his days, Frederick could not help but wonder who betrayed them. Was it really Jenkins, or someone else?

Thomas Auld arrived soon afterward to take the four other men home. But he left Frederick in jail. Frederick was not happy, but deep down he understood Auld's actions. After all, Frederick had been the ringleader of the escape attempt.[3]

Frederick languished in the county jail not knowing what would happen. Finally, after a week, Thomas Auld released him. He told Frederick that he planned to sell him to a friend in Alabama. William Hambleton made a scarier threat. Hambleton told Frederick he would shoot him if Auld did not send him out of the area.

Auld did not follow through on his threat. Some historians think he did not even have a friend in Alabama. It seemed that he wanted to frighten Frederick so he would never again try to escape.[4] Many historians think Auld did not send Frederick to Alabama because deep down he liked Frederick. He even considered him a member of his family.

Learning a Trade

Auld thought it would be best for Frederick to learn a skill. In the spring of 1836, Frederick was sent once again to live with Thomas's brother, Hugh, in Baltimore. Life was different there for Frederick than when he lived with Hugh's family three years earlier. Hugh's son, Thomas, no longer wanted to be friends with a slave. Hugh's wife, Sophia, was not as close to

Frederick as before. Frederick was now eighteen and no longer an adolescent. He was more independent than when he last lived with the Aulds.

Hugh Auld's shipbuilding business had gone bankrupt since Frederick had first lived with him. So Hugh arranged for Frederick to work as an apprentice caulker in a shipyard owned by William Gardiner. Frederick adjusted to the work with ease. However, some of the ships he helped build were used in slave trade between the states.

The greatest threats to his enjoyment were white coworkers. Many were Irish immigrants. They were largely uneducated and poor. To these immigrants, the slaves and free blacks who worked alongside them were competitors for their jobs.[5] It was only natural that tensions would boil over. Fights constantly broke out.

A Brutal Fight

One day, four white workers ganged up on Frederick. Three of the men beat him with bricks and bars. A fourth crept up from behind and hit Frederick over the head with a metal bar. Frederick fell to the ground. As he tried to get up, the four men continued to beat and kick him. One kicked him in his eye, causing it to bleed and swell shut. Other white workers cheered on the attackers.

Frederick staggered home. Sophia Auld was heartbroken to see Frederick battered and bloody. She tenderly dressed his wounds. Hugh was furious with the attackers. Some of his anger may have been because

When Frederick was an apprentice caulker, he worked in the shipyards of Baltimore. This 1840 engraving of a New York shipyard is the type of place where Frederick worked.

he cared about Frederick as a person. On the other hand, some of it could have been because Frederick, his property, had been damaged.

Hugh Auld tried to press charges against the workers. A judge asked him if he had witnessed the fight. Auld answered that he did not. He added, however, that many workers at the shipyard did see the entire assault. The judge said that in Maryland that did not matter because the workers would not testify. In Maryland, a black person could not bring evidence against whites unless he or she had whites as witnesses on his or her behalf. Since there were no whites who would testify against the four men, the judge was forced to drop the case. Auld and Frederick learned a valuable lesson about the Maryland justice system before the Civil War.

Auld was so angry that he took Frederick away from Gardiner's shipyard. He brought Frederick to work at a shipyard owned by a man named Asa Price. Since Auld worked as a foreman at Price's shipyard, he could keep an eye on Frederick to be sure he was not abused.

A Bit More Freedom

Frederick worked out a deal with Auld that allowed him more freedom. He would officially still be a slave, but he would find his own work and collect his own wages. He would give Auld $3 a week, about $51.56 today.[6] Even if he did not earn any money during a particular week, he still owed Auld the three dollars. Frederick would also arrange his own room and board. Deals like this were not unusual for slaves and their owners in Baltimore.

Frederick was delighted with this arrangement. He could work when he wanted and earn more money. He wrote: "I was ready to work by night as by day, and being in the possession of excellent health, I was not only able to meet my current expenses, but also to lay by a small sum at the end of each week.[7]

This arrangement gave Frederick new opportunities. He took a job escorting a child to school. Around the same time, he founded a debating club with five free African Americans. They called it the East Baltimore Mental Improvement Society. The group met at different members' houses and discussed topics ranging from African-American life to religion. The society also held social gatherings.

Meeting Anna

At one of these social events, Frederick met a free African-American woman named Anna Murray. Anna was a talented violinist. In time, they got to know each other and soon were involved romantically. Because Anna was one of twelve children, she was forced to learn domestic skills. By the time she was seventeen, Anna was working as a housekeeper for a family.

The more time Frederick spent with the East Baltimore Mental Improvement Society the better he became at debating. By listening to other educated African Americans, he became more and more determined in his attitudes about slavery. His arrangement with Hugh Auld permitted him a lot of freedom in his daily life. Still, Frederick legally remained a slave. Auld could change his mind about the agreement at any time. If either Hugh or Thomas Auld should die, Frederick's future was uncertain.

On one summer day in 1838, Frederick was about to leave for a weekend religious and social retreat. He planned to pay Hugh Auld his weekly three dollars the Saturday before he left. Due to a delay at the shipyard, Frederick did not pay Auld before leaving for the conference. He was scheduled to return on Sunday. But he had such a good time at the conference that he stayed overnight on Sunday. Auld was furious when Frederick showed up on Monday to pay him.

Auld did not like getting his money two days late. He was also outraged that Frederick left town without his approval. A heated argument broke out between

Anna Murray was a talented violinist when she met Frederick.

slave and owner. Frederick said that he never knew that he needed Auld's permission to go where he wanted to. In the heat of anger, Auld threatened to whip Frederick. Auld did not whip him, however, he did end the arrangement that allowed Frederick independence.

Another Escape Try

Over the next three weeks, Frederick planned another escape. He would use train and steamboat travel to head to the nearest free northern city, Philadelphia.

But how would he get on board undetected? As an African-American man in Maryland, he needed a special identification paper to prove he was not a slave. Frederick made the acquaintance of a retired African-American merchant sailor named Stanley. It was Stanley who gave Frederick the paper identifying him as a retired sailor, giving him seaman's protection.

There was no guarantee this identification paper would work. Frederick did not resemble the much-older Stanley. On the other hand, working in shipyards had turned Frederick into a maritime expert. He could answer any question about ships asked by a doubtful train conductor.

There was another problem. Frederick could not afford a train ticket. Anna solved that problem for him. She sold a feather bed and gave Frederick the money from the sale. Some believe she may have taken money out of her own savings to help Frederick buy a ticket. The plans were for Frederick to send for Anna after he reached safety in the North. Then they would get married.

It was then that Frederick embarked on his nerve-racking escape from Maryland to Philadelphia. However, his final goal was New York City. He boarded a train for New York a few hours after he arrived in Philadelphia. Frederick arrived in New York City, exhausted but thrilled, around 1 A.M.

A New Life in New Bedford

As he walked up and down the busy streets of New York, Frederick basked in his newfound freedom. He wrote: "The bonds that had held me to 'old master' were broken. No man now had a right to call me his slave or assert mastery over me."[1] He wrote to a friend: "I felt as one might feel upon escape from a den of hungry lions."[2]

His happiness did not last long. Soon after arriving, he met a fugitive slave he had known in Baltimore. As a slave, he was known by the name of Allender's Jake. In New York, he had taken a formal name, William Dixon. He told Frederick he must be careful. New York was filled with people trying to capture fugitive slaves. Some were native southerners. Some were even African Americans willing to betray slaves to make some money. Dixon warned Frederick not to trust a soul in New York.

David Ruggles

Frederick was terrified about being discovered.[3] His plans were to go to the house of David Ruggles, leader of a group called the Vigilance Committee. The committee protected escaped slaves in New York and helped them relocate to safe places. Frederick was not sure where Ruggles lived. After talking to Dixon, he was scared to ask anyone he met for directions.

He spent a few more days wandering the streets. One night, he slept behind some barrels stacked on a wharf. Hungry and homeless, Frederick finally spoke to a sailor he met. The sailor was friendly and took Frederick to his home for the night. The next day, he brought Frederick to Ruggles's house.

Ruggles welcomed the ex-slave and suggested that he move to New England. There were less risks there for former slaves. New Bedford, Massachusetts, was the whaling capital of New England. Ships were constantly sailing to and from New Bedford. So there would be many chances for Frederick to find work. To make it a bit harder for slave hunters to find him, Frederick changed his name to Frederick Johnson.

Marriage

Before he moved to New Bedford, Frederick had some unfinished business to tend to. He wrote to Anna Murray and urged her to travel to New York. Since Anna was a free African American, she had official papers and made the trip without a problem. On September 15, 1838, Frederick met her in New York where the two married.

The newly married couple headed to Massachusetts. Ruggles had made arrangements with friends in New Bedford to take care of Frederick and Anna Johnson. By coincidence, the friends were also named Johnson— Nathan and Mary Johnson. They were a free African-American couple.

New Bedford was filled with citizens named Johnson. Frederick felt he wanted a more distinctive name, and he allowed Nathan Johnson to choose it. However, Frederick "told him he must not take from me the name of 'Frederick.' I must hold on to that, to preserve a sense of my identity."[4]

Named for a Poem's Character

At the time, Nathan Johnson was reading a classic poem titled "Lady of the Lake." Scottish author and poet Sir Walter Scott wrote it in 1810. Two main characters are a father and daughter with the last name Douglas. Nathan suggested that name, and Frederick liked the sound of it. Frederick added an extra *s* because some important African-American families in Baltimore and

Philadelphia were named Douglass. There were no more name changes for the former slave. He would forever be known as Frederick Douglass.

The Douglasses settled smoothly into New Bedford life. They must have been given money since Douglass had none of his own.[5] More than likely, the Underground Railroad helped him out.[6] The Douglasses rented a house. Then Douglass took odd jobs to earn money. He shoveled coal for a minister's house. Coal was a much-used fuel for keeping buildings warm. Another job was sawing wood to be used to heat ships sailing out of New Bedford.

Frederick Douglass was a skilled caulker, however. It was a waste of his talent to only shovel coal and saw wood. He was hired as a ship caulker in a boatyard owned by a man named Rodney French. Douglass's pay would be $2 a day, worth about $36.53 today.[7] It does not sound like a lot of money, but then it was a healthy income.

As soon as Douglass reported to work, whites told him they would not work alongside a black man.[8] The North may have been free of slavery, but it was not free of prejudice or racism. So Douglass was forced to go back to shoveling coal and sawing wood. The pay was half the money he could have earned as a caulker. Meanwhile, Anna worked as a maid and a laundress.

Prejudice at Church

The Douglasses planned to attend church regularly. They first went to services at the Elm Street Methodist

Church. The congregation was mostly white, but the church allowed black worshippers to attend as well. However, once Douglass set foot inside the church, he saw that prejudice was alive and well there, too. Blacks had to sit in a gallery in the back, separate from the white congregants.

The attitude of the minister, Isaac Bonney, was just as troubling. The white congregants took communion first. When they finished, Bonney looked toward the back of the church. He called out to the African Americans, "Come up, colored friends, come up, for you know God is no respecter of persons."[9] Douglass thought Bonney was talking down to the African-American worshippers. He never again set foot in the Elm Street Methodist Church.

Douglass then found the Zion Chapel. It was affiliated with the African Methodist Episcopal (AME), an offshoot of the Methodist church. Black Methodists founded the AME denomination in the eighteenth century. It was a response to prejudice they felt existed in the mostly white Methodist churches.

The Liberator

One day in New Bedford, a young newspaper peddler approached Douglass. The man was selling a newspaper called *The Liberator*. It had a strong abolitionist point of view. *The Liberator* was published by the American Anti-Slavery Society. Its publisher was William Lloyd Garrison, a white man. Douglass bought a copy and began reading it frequently. Douglass wrote: "The paper became my meat and drink. My soul was set all on fire."[10]

As with many active churchgoers, Douglass found a second home in the Zion Chapel. On March 12, 1839, he gave a powerful talk at a church meeting. One solution to the slavery issue being discussed at the time was called colonization. That meant sending slaves and other African Americans back to Africa where they or their ancestors had come from. Douglass blasted the idea. He said that slaves should be set free as American citizens and allowed to stay in the United States. Garrison heard about Douglass's comments and reported them in *The Liberator.*

Shortly afterward, Douglass heard Garrison speak for the first time. On April 16, 1839, Garrison addressed a group of white and black supporters in New

Bedford. Garrison preached strict nonviolence. He stated that people who claimed to be Christians but supported slavery were hypocrites. He used biblical references in his talk, and that impressed Douglass.[11] Garrison stated that "prejudice against color was rebellion against God."[12]

In the meantime, the Douglass family began to grow. Their first child, a daughter they named Rosetta, was born on June 24, 1839. Their son, Lewis Henry, was born on October 9, 1840.

A Major Trip to Nantucket

In the middle of August 1841, Douglass took advantage of an opportunity to become better known. He sailed to the island of Nantucket to attend a meeting of the Massachusetts Anti-Slavery Society. Today, Nantucket

The Liberator *was one of Frederick Douglass's first inspirations to join the abolitionist fight. Left, is part of the paper's July 24, 1868 edition. This portion of a newspaper is called the masthead.*

William Lloyd Garrison

William Lloyd Garrison was an odd-looking man. He was bald, had a hawklike nose, and wore glasses. Yet those who heard him speak were drawn to him. Garrison was born December 12, 1805, in Newburyport, Massachusetts, near the New Hampshire border. He started working as a writer and editor for a newspaper called the *Newburyport Herald* when he was twelve. It was at the *Herald* that he received the training he would need to publish his own paper.

In 1828, Garrison met a strong Quaker abolitionist named Benjamin Lundy, who had lived for a while in the South. Lundy told Garrison about the cruelties of slavery. His tales were enough to lead Garrison to join the abolitionist movement. Garrison published his first copy of *The Liberator* on January 1, 1831. He urged the immediate freeing of all slaves. That was a radical view in the early 1830s, and not just in the South. Northerners who opposed slavery had problems with Garrison's ideas. They felt there was no way so many freed slaves could find jobs and become working members of society at one time.

is best known as a resort island. But in the 1840s, a lot of abolitionists lived there. Many were Quakers, who were strongly against slavery. The antislavery group was sure to find a friendly reception.

Some of the best known abolitionists were there. That included Garrison himself. Others were Wendell Phillips, New Hampshire-based abolitionist Parker Pillsbury, and local leader John A. Collins.

Douglass only planned to be a spectator. However, one of the group's leaders, William C. Coffin, had heard Douglass speak in the Zion Chapel. Coffin invited Douglass to address the Nantucket crowd.

This would be Douglass's first speech in front of an audience of strangers. Douglass admitted he was nervous.[13] As he started talking, he seemed confused. He stammered as he discussed life as a slave. As he continued, Douglass gained more confidence. He spoke in a clear and powerful voice as he recounted his escape from slavery. Douglass's story fascinated the audience.

Parker Pillsbury said of Douglass, "[T]hough it was late in the evening when the young man closed his remarks, none seemed to know or care for the hour."[14] Garrison compared Douglass to the great Revolutionary War-era orator Patrick Henry, who had given the famous "Give me liberty or give me death" speech. Garrison said, beaming, "Patrick Henry had never made a more eloquent speech than the one they had just listened to from the lips of the hunted fugitive."[15]

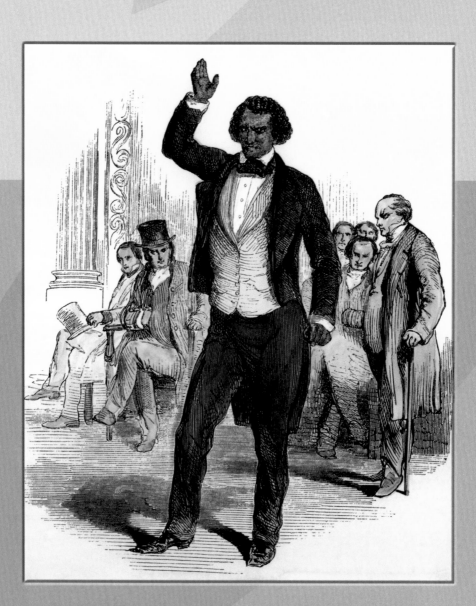

Frederick Douglass proved to be a great speaker. He often discussed what he had experienced as a slave.

Being Paid to Speak

Douglass was asked if he would become a regular paid lecturer for Garrison's American Anti-Slavery Society. Though Douglass never had a formal education, he agreed to give it a try for three months.

Douglass lasted more than three months. For the rest of 1841, he lectured in eastern Massachusetts and neighboring Rhode Island on behalf of the American Anti-Slavery Society. That was a major feat considering that he had been a slave just a few years earlier.

His new role meant another move for the Douglass family. In the fall of 1841, they moved to Lynn, Massachusetts. Lynn is about seventy miles north of New Bedford. It had a large Quaker population. Since Lynn is only about ten miles from Boston, Douglass could always make a short train trip to see Garrison for business meetings. The Douglasses settled into their home alongside the railroad tracks in Lynn.

6

"As a Speaker, He Has Few Equals"

L ynn may have been one of the friendlier towns for African Americans in the early 1840s. Yet Frederick Douglass soon learned that, like New Bedford, not all people in Lynn were free of prejudice. One day in September 1841, Douglass and John Collins boarded a train together. They were on their way to an abolitionist meeting in Dover, New Hampshire.

A conductor approached the two men and told Douglass he had to move to the car for African

Americans. Douglass refused. The conductor called for help and a few men arrived. They dragged Douglass from his seat and also roughed up Collins.

Later that month, the same thing happened again on the same train. This time, Douglass grabbed the seat and refused to let go. After all the years of working on the docks of Baltimore and New Bedford, Douglass had strong arms. The conductor and his crew could not move Douglass. They gave up, and Douglass stayed in his seat until the train arrived at its destination.

Boycott

After hearing how Douglass had been treated, abolitionists threatened to boycott, or stop riding, that railroad. The railroad owners did not seem to mind. Maybe they figured they would rather lose money than fairly accommodate African Americans. Or perhaps they thought there were not enough black riders and their supporters for a boycott to affect the railroad business. In response to the boycott, the owners ordered their trains not to stop to pick up or discharge passengers in Lynn if Douglass was there. They also forced other free black men to sit in a car only for blacks. Arguments and fights then broke out between conductors and black men and their white friends. To end the violence, the rule of having a separate car for blacks was lifted. The boycott worked.

The Douglasses welcomed another member to their family on March 3, 1842. Son Frederick, Jr., was the couple's third child. However, Douglass's growing family did not stop him from traveling to talk to audiences. He had plenty to speak about.

Entrancing Speaker

Douglass engaged his audiences with true tales of horrors he witnessed as a slave. Audiences were especially moved when Douglass mentioned beatings given to children and elderly people. One incident he related was about a young girl who had been beaten. He had touched her head and found it "nearly covered with festering sores."[1]

He also criticized citizens of the North. Douglass remarked that while no slavery existed in Massachusetts, he was not treated as an equal in his new home state. He used the train incidents as examples. He also told how he could not take a job as a caulker in New Bedford because whites would not work alongside him.

Douglass used humor in his lectures too. He would imitate Christian ministers who told slaves that disobeying their owners offended God.

Douglass's audiences warmed to the former slave. He had a commanding stage presence. Douglass spoke with a baritone voice and stood tall and sturdy. With his mass of black hair and intense eyes, Douglass was hard to ignore. One newspaper, the

Elisha Hammond painted this oil portrait of a young Frederick Douglass in 1844.

Herald of Freedom based in Concord, Massachusetts, wrote: "As a speaker, he has few equals."[2]

His speeches were especially important since a lot of proslavery publications were now being distributed in the North. The articles in these publications stated that slaves had fairly easy lives. Some added that many slaves lived better than poor whites. They concluded that slaves were very pleased with their lives in the South. Douglass's true stories countered the lies being published in the proslavery journals.

Garrison gave Douglass permission to lecture on behalf of the American Anti-Slavery Society outside of New England. That brought new challenges. In what was then referred to as the Western states (today the American Midwest), many more residents were sympathetic to slave owners than in New England.

A Rough Time in Indiana

On September 16, 1843, Douglass and two other abolitionists were in Pendleton, Indiana. They were about to conduct a meeting outdoors with about one hundred other abolitionists. A gang of anti-abolitionists showed up. They surrounded the abolitionists and threw rocks and rotten eggs at them. One man in the anti-abolitionist mob grabbed the speaker's wooden platform and broke it into pieces. Douglass tried to abide by Garrison's code of nonviolence. But when he saw the mob threaten fellow abolitionist leader William White, Douglass grabbed a piece of wood to use as a weapon.

In doing so, he broke not only Garrison's code but also a real law. Indiana law stated that blacks could not raise weapons against whites. Mob members threatened to kill Douglass. Douglass ran with his enemies in pursuit. One took a club and whacked Douglass in the hand. Douglass's bones shattered and he fell to the ground. Nearby was William White, bleeding from his mouth. The attackers left on horseback.

Supporters helped Douglass and White into a wagon and took them to one of their homes. Douglass's hand never healed correctly. It caused him pain the rest of his life.

There were scares like that during many of Douglass's talks in that part of the country. Still, Douglass and his fellow abolitionists felt they must get their antislavery message out.

Speaking as an activist did not earn much money. Back in Lynn, Anna Douglass earned some income sewing shoes. Because she had small children, it is believed she worked at home and not in a factory. Meanwhile, Frederick Douglass continued lecturing well into 1844. On October 21 that year, his fourth child was born—a son named Charles Remond Douglass. It was in honor of Douglass's friend, Charles Remond.

Douglass's speaking ability and intelligence caused an unforeseen problem. Because it was illegal in the South to teach slaves to read and write, many slaves and former slaves were illiterate. Those who could read or write had only the most basic skills. Douglass told audiences that he had been a free man only a few years, and he never had a formal education. Some people

Frederick Douglass fights off a mob with clubs in Indiana.

Charles Remond

Charles Lenox Remond—a free African-American man born in Salem, Massachusetts, in 1810—is regarded as the first African American to speak publicly on abolition. Like Douglass, Remond was very close to William Lloyd Garrison. He traveled to London with Garrison to attend the World's Anti-Slavery Convention in 1840. Following the convention, he stayed in the British Isles for more than a year and a half to lecture on abolitionism.

A member of the Massachusetts Anti-Slavery Society, Remond was not as powerful a speaker as Douglass. However, he was popular and became known as a witty and determined speaker. He and Douglass both agreed that African Americans should stop attending any church that discriminated against them in any way. Remond died in 1878.

found his story difficult to accept. They started to believe he was a fake, and that he made up his story about his life as a slave.

Putting It Down on Paper

The best way for Douglass to fight this problem was to tell his story in writing. In the winter of 1844, he started to write his autobiography. Garrison's American Anti-Slavery Society published the book in May 1845. Douglass titled it *Narrative of the Life of Frederick Douglass, An American Slave, Written by Himself.*

The book received rave reviews. A critic for Douglass's hometown newspaper, *The Lynn Pioneer*, wrote: "It is the most thrilling work which the American press has ever issued—and the most important. If it does not open the eyes of this people, they must be petrified into eternal sleep."[3]

Douglass's autobiography sold very well. But while it solved one problem, it created another. Because the book was so popular, more people than ever became aware that he was an escaped slave. That could have included his owner, Thomas Auld. If Douglass was captured, he could be legally returned to Auld.

England Bound

Douglass decided the wisest thing to do was to leave the country. In August 1845, he boarded a ship bound for England. With slavery illegal in England since 1838, Douglass hoped the British would support the American abolition movement.

Since Douglass had by now achieved some fame, the ship captain asked him to give a speech on the last evening of the voyage. Douglass did so. He also took advantage of the opportunity to strongly criticize ship-owners who illegally transported Africans to the United States to be used as slaves. (The international slave trade had been banned in the United States in 1808.)

A few passengers who had been drinking tried to shout down Douglass. In response, the captain threat-ened to lock the hecklers in irons as ship prisoners if they continued to hassle Douglass. Some versions of the story say that the captain actually punched one of the drunken men in the face. There were no more problems during the remainder of the trip.

A Warm Welcome in Ireland

Douglass spent the rest of 1845 speaking throughout Ireland. As he had hoped, he was mostly welcomed with open arms. Early in 1846, he sailed to Scotland. Later that year, he traveled through England, giving speeches. The overall lack of bigotry Douglass encountered impressed him. He wrote that in the British Isles he was treated "not as a color, but as a man."[4]

Despite that, Douglass was homesick. On April 16, he wrote to William Lloyd Garrison:

I long to be home—'home, sweet, sweet home! Be it ever so humble, there is no place like home.' Nor is it merely to enjoy the pleasure of family and friends, that I wish to be at home: it is to be in the field, at work, preaching to the best of my ability salvation from slavery, to a nation fast hastening to destruction.[5]

Teaming Up Again With Garrison

In the summer of 1846, Garrison sailed to England and met Douglass. They traveled Great Britain making speeches together. And they were not scared to take on local targets. Some people who donated money to support the Free Church of Scotland were Americans of Scottish descent. Many were slaveholders. Douglass and Garrison publicly urged the church to return money they received from slaveholders. The church never did so, but the campaign brought the abolitionist movement great publicity.

Douglass enjoyed mocking people in his speeches who claimed to be Christians but did not act like them. In Sheffield, England, on September 12, 1846, Douglass imitated a preacher telling slaves to obey their owners. He jokingly said, "You should obey your masters . . . because of the sense of gratitude with which you should be inspired by the knowledge of the fact that God has brought you in his great mercy from Africa to this country."[6]

To such preachers, slave sellers did a good thing by taking Africans from their godless world and bringing them to the United States where they could be both Christians and obedient slaves. As Douglass exposed this foolish thinking, the British audience roared in laughter.

Well into the fall, Douglass ached to return to the United States. Garrison and some of Douglass's coworkers asked him to stay for another six months. Some wanted Douglass to settle permanently in England. But Douglass knew he had to return to the United States where slavery remained a burning issue.[7] That was despite the fact that he could be captured.

Finally, Officially Free

Garrison left England in October 1846, but Douglass stayed a few more months. In early December, he was in the city of Newcastle upon Tyne where he stayed with a family named Richardson. The Richardsons were Quakers and devout abolitionists. One family member, Ellen Richardson, had an idea that would solve Douglass's concern about being captured in the United States. She offered to buy him from Thomas Auld.

Richardson did not have enough money to buy Douglass so she asked other abolitionists for donations. Auld wanted about 150 British pounds, which was equal to $1,250 in American money at the time.[8] That is worth $26,113 today.[9] Richardson was able to collect the money. She paid Auld, and, as of December 12, 1846, Frederick Douglass was a free man.

Christmas in England

Douglass spent Christmas Day at the Richardsons' house. While there, he met a fiery British abolitionist named Julia Griffiths. The two connected right away and would become friends for the rest of their lives.

Douglass returned to the United States in the spring of 1847. He sailed into Boston, where a group of admirers met him. But Douglass was anxious to see his family. He immediately took a train to Lynn. As soon as he stepped out of the train, he saw his sons running to meet him. He picked up one son and took the other by the hand. He then entered his home for the first time in nearly two years.

This early type of photograph, called a daguerreotype, was taken of Douglass in 1847.

His family and friends were delighted to see him. However, Douglass discovered that some former friends were disappointed in him. They were angry that he allowed a friend to buy his freedom. By having a person—even a friend—purchase his freedom, he seemed to admit that a man has the legal right to own another man.

Douglass answered that he did not view Thomas Auld as his owner. He said Auld was a kidnapper and the money Richardson paid was ransom. William Lloyd Garrison defended Douglass. That silenced some, but not all, of his critics. Douglass historian Frank Faragasso offers this explanation, "Having his freedom purchased was something that he could not turn down. Freedom is the highest goal. It is hard to understand what this meant to Douglass. He would not turn down such an opportunity."[10]

His Own North Star

Douglass returned home restless. He had big plans, including starting his own abolitionist newspaper. As owner of his own paper, he would not have to get approval on what to write as he did with Garrison's paper, *The Liberator*. He also believed it was very important for African Americans to be able to speak for themselves with their own publications.

Garrison and other abolitionists were unhappy with Douglass's plans. Some thought Douglass should continue lecturing where he had a great impact. There was also a business concern. Another antislavery newspaper would compete for the same readers as Garrison's *The Liberator*. Garrison never got rich publishing *The Liberator*. He often struggled to find the money to keep his newspaper going.

Yet Douglass had his mind made up, and that hurt Garrison. He said of Douglass, "Such conduct grieves me to the heart."[1]

The North Star

It would have been hard for Douglass to stay in Boston where he was close to Garrison. Douglass decided to move his family to the city of Rochester in western New York state. Rochester is about four hundred miles from Boston. In the 1840s, it was home to many abolitionists and other reformers. These included supporters of woman suffrage, or the right of women to vote. It seemed like a place where an activist like Douglass could feel at home. Douglass bought a printing press and hired a staff. He published the first edition of his newspaper on December 3, 1847.

Douglass called his newspaper *The North Star*. The title had to do with the Underground Railroad.

The North Star's slogan was "Right is of no Sex— Truth is of no Color—God is the Father of us all, and we are all Brethren."[2] Douglass also published his intent in *The North Star*. He printed important words in capital letters: "The object of the North Star will be to attack SLAVERY in all its forms and aspects; advocate

The Underground Railroad

The Underground Railroad was not an actual railroad. It was the informal name for a network of places where escaped slaves could stay while heading north to freedom. Even after reaching a free state, they were still in danger of bounty hunters. Often the final destination was Canada. In Canada, slavery was illegal. In addition, the fugitive slave laws of the United States did not apply in Canada.

Escaping slaves lacked maps and compasses. But they had to find a way to be certain they were heading north. So they looked to the skies and used the North Star as a guide. As long as they followed the North Star, they knew they were on the right path. Since the North Star was so important for escaped slaves, it made a perfect name for Douglass's newspaper.

Some communities known for being havens on the Underground Railroad included big cities such as Chicago and Cincinnati and small towns like Ripley, Ohio, and Farmington, Connecticut. Famous hiding places ranged from a dugout room below a cabin owned by the Mayhew family in Nebraska to the attic of Bialystoker Synagogue in New York City.

UNIVERSAL EMANCIPATION; exalt the standard of PUBLIC MORALS; promote the moral and intellectual improvement of the COLORED PEOPLE; and hasten the day of FREEDOM to the THREE MILLION of our ENSLAVED FELLOW COUNTRYMEN."[3]

The North Star ran four pages, and Douglass sent copies to Canada, Australia, Great Britain, and Mexico as well as much of the United States. He even had subscribers in states where slavery was legal.

The Move West

In February 1848, Douglass returned to Lynn to help his family move. He brought them to their new home in Rochester. Their house had a small garden that Anna liked to tend. But she had little to do with Frederick's abolitionist friends he hosted at their house. Historian Frank Faragasso says, "Frederick offered to teach Anna to read and he tried to hire a tutor as well. But she would have none of it. She saw her role as homemaker and mother and she wanted to stay out of public life."[4]

On July 19 and 20, 1848, Douglass attended a meeting along with three hundred men and women in the village of Seneca Falls, about fifty miles east of Rochester. The meeting had been organized by a small group of women led by Lucretia Mott and Elizabeth Cady Stanton. Douglass proved that his interests in helping others went beyond African Americans. On those two summer days, Seneca Falls served as the setting for the first women's rights convention in the United States.

The North Star *was Frederick Douglass's voice for his abolitionist views.*

The most important result of the convention was the drafting of a document called the Declaration of Sentiments. It was based on the Declaration of Independence. The Declaration of Sentiments called for basic rights for women. These included the right for women to own property and the right for married women to keep wages they earned. At the time, any money married women earned went right to their husbands.

Historian Anne Derousie said:

Douglass printed up the minutes and printed the Declaration of Sentiments as a pamphlet to be distributed. But his most important act at the convention was speaking in favor of the suffrage

plank in the Declaration of Sentiments. Some people at the convention thought asking for the right to vote was asking for too much. But Douglass said that the right to vote is the necessary beginning of all rights.[5]

A Long Distance Letter to Thomas Auld

Back home, Douglass continued to spend most of his time on his newspaper. September 1848 marked the tenth anniversary of his escape from Thomas Auld. He used the occasion to publish a personal letter to Auld in *The North Star*. It was titled: "Letter to His Old Master."

Frederick and Anna Douglass settled in Rochester, New York.

In it, Douglass told Auld about the last ten years of his life. At one point in the letter, Douglass told Auld he is now married and has four children. He contrasted his children's future with those of slave children. Douglass wrote:

> *These dear children are ours—not to work up into rice, sugar, and tobacco, but to watch over, regard, and protect, and to rear them up in the nurture and admonition of the gospel—to train them up in the paths of wisdom and virtue, and, as far as we can, to make them useful to the world and to themselves. Oh! sir, a slaveholder never appears to me so completely an agent of hell, as when I think of and look upon my dear children.*[6]

Yet he concluded his letter saying, "There is no roof under which you would be more safe than mine, and there is nothing in my house which you might need for your comfort, which I would not readily grant. Indeed, I should esteem it a privilege to set you an example as to how mankind ought to treat each other. I am your fellow-man, but not your slave."[7]

Douglass was by now famous throughout much of the world. His autobiography, *Narrative of the Life of Frederick Douglass, An American Slave, Written by Himself,* had sold eleven thousand copies.[8]

Unfairness in the Schools

Despite the respect his book gave him, Douglass learned again that in the eyes of many white people he remained inferior. As in New Bedford and Lynn, Douglass found prejudice in Rochester. In 1849, his oldest daughter, Rosetta, was ready to go to school. Douglass learned that public schools in Rochester did not accept African-American children. He arranged for Rosetta to attend a private school.

In the private school, Rosetta was forced to sit separately from the white students. There was no way Douglass would stand for his daughter being treated as anything but equal. He took her out of the school and hired a woman to teach Rosetta at home. As a result of this issue, Douglass now had a new campaign—to abolish segregation in Rochester's public schools.

He also welcomed yet another member of the family. On March 22, 1849, Anna Douglass gave birth to a daughter, Annie—the last of the Douglass children.

Meanwhile, Douglass's pet project, *The North Star,* struggled. Douglass realized he and his small staff could not run the newspaper alone. He hired his British friend Julia Griffiths to help out. Griffiths and her sister Eliza arrived from Britain in the spring of 1849.

Raised Eyebrows

Griffiths was a smart woman with a strong business sense. She filled two roles at *The North Star.* She worked as an editor, helping Douglass prepare articles for publication. Yet she also raised necessary money to keep the paper alive.

She and Douglass raised eyebrows when the two appeared together in public. While today most people do not think twice when seeing a black man and a white woman together, that was not the case in 1850. Gossipers including William Lloyd Garrison spread rumors that Douglass and Griffiths were a romantic couple, despite the fact that Douglass was married. On one occasion in 1850, Douglass and Julia and Eliza Giffiths were walking together down a street in New York City. A mob of white men spotted the three friends. Angry at the sight of a black man with two white women, they ganged up on Douglass and beat him. The Griffiths sisters found a policeman, who stopped the attackers.

His Own Underground Railroad Station

Concerning abolition, Douglass believed in the saying that actions speak louder than words. The Douglass family home and his office became stops on the Underground Railroad. Rochester is a port city on the south shore of one of the Great Lakes, Lake Ontario. On the north shore of the lake is Canada. Escaped slaves had easy access by boat to Canada and safety. It is believed that between 150 and 300 slaves passed through Rochester each year while the Underground Railroad existed.[9] Then, in the fall of 1850, the U.S. government took a step backward in the fight to abolish slavery. The U.S. Congress passed the Fugitive Slave Act.

Douglass attended the American Anti-Slavery Society annual meeting in May 1851. It was there that he met his old friend, William Lloyd Garrison. If their fellow abolitionists expected Douglass and Garrison to patch up their differences they were disappointed. Douglass angered Garrison by announcing that he supported the U.S. Constitution. Douglass publicly said that according to the Constitution, slavery was illegal. Garrison had always stated that according to his interpretation, the document was proslavery.

Douglass felt that abolitionists needed to be more active. He asked the readers of *The North Star* to enter politics. By entering politics, they would become lawmakers. As lawmakers, they could help pass antislavery laws.

Garrison did not like that idea either. Garrison and his supporters felt Americans would come to their senses and accept the basic idea that slavery was evil. Douglass thought that was naive. After the meeting, articles in Garrison's newspaper attacked Douglass. The split between the two former friends had deepened.

The next month, Douglass took a bold stand. He changed the name of *The North Star* to *Frederick*

The Fugitive Slave Act and the Compromise of 1850

From 1846 to 1848 the United States was at war with Mexico. When the Mexican War ended, the United States controlled land that had been part of Mexico. Lawmakers in the South wanted slavery to be legal on that land. Northerners, naturally, wanted slavery outlawed there.

In 1850, Congress tried to make both sides happy. To satisfy abolitionists, Congress banned the slave trade in Washington, D.C. Congress also admitted California to the union as a free state.

To satisfy proslavery people, land obtained in the Mexican War would become the Utah and New Mexico territories. The people living in each territory would decide whether or not slavery would be legal in their territories.

Congress also passed a stricter fugitive slave law. The old fugitive slave law from 1793 stated that runaway slaves were the property of their owners even if they had escaped to land where slavery was outlawed. Slave owners had long complained that the first law was hard to enforce. The stricter 1850 fugitive slave law allowed federal agents to track down and arrest runaway slaves anywhere in the United States. It also made it a crime to give safe haven to fugitive slaves.

This entire set of new laws was known as the Compromise of 1850. Historians believe it delayed the Civil War for ten years. Regardless, Douglass and his friends were outraged by the tougher fugitive slave law. In response, Douglass lost faith in the current members of Congress and began to look at different ways to abolish slavery.

Douglass' Paper. Douglass said he wanted to make his paper stand out against so many other newspapers with the word *Star* in their names.

A Different View of the Fourth of July

Douglass gave one of his most famous speeches on July 5, 1852. It was titled: "What to the Slave Is the Fourth of July?" The setting was Corinthian Hall in Rochester. The speech attacked inequality between the races in the United States. The purpose was to show how a slave viewed one of the grandest American holidays. It was filled with references to God and the nation.

Douglass said in part:

What, to the American slave, is your 4th of July? I answer; a day that reveals to him, more than all other days in the year, the gross injustice and cruelty to which he is the constant victim. To him, your celebration is a sham; your boasted liberty, an unholy license; your national greatness, swelling vanity; your sounds of rejoicing are empty and heartless; your denunciation of tyrants, brass fronted impudence; your shouts of liberty and equality, hollow mockery; your prayers and hymns, your sermons and thanksgivings, with all your religious parade and solemnity, are, to Him, mere bombast, fraud, deception, impiety, and hypocrisy—a thin veil to cover up crimes which would disgrace a nation of savages. There is not a nation on the earth guilty of practices more shocking and bloody than are the people of the United States, at this very hour.[10]

When he finished talking, the audience stood and cheered. They fully understood Douglass's anger. Even today, Douglass's July 5 speech is regarded as one of he greatest in American history.

Douglass's Next Autobiography

Douglass, meanwhile, continued writing. He composed his second autobiography, published in 1855. Its title was *My Bondage and My Freedom.* And Douglass met one of his goals in 1857, when the city of Rochester outlawed segregation in its public schools.

Although the antisegregation decision in Rochester in 1857 made Douglass happy, a decision that year by the U.S. Supreme Court angered him A slave named Dred Scott lived with his owner Dr. John Emerson in the slave state of Missouri. Emerson was a surgeon in the Army, so he often traveled. When he did, he took Scott with him. Twice Emerson took Scott to places where slavery was illegal: the state of Illinois and the territory of Wisconsin. Scott claimed that when he lived in places where slavery was banned, he could no longer be a slave. He said living in Illinois and Wisconsin made him a free man.

The Supreme Court disagreed with Scott. Chief Justice Roger Taney indicated that the framers of the Constitution intended that blacks, whether slaves or

Ezra Greenleaf Weld took this daguerreotype of Douglass (seated to left of table) and others at the Fugitive Slave Law Convention at Cazenovia, New York, on August 22, 1850.

not, did not have the rights of whites. Historian Margaret Washington said:

> If the fugitive slave law politicized Douglass, Dred Scott radicalized him. Basically what the decision said [to African Americans] was that you're not a citizen, you will never be. . . . And this is coming from the highest law in the land, the Constitution. So what else is open to a black man except radical resistance.[11]

Douglass no longer ruled out violence as a possible way to end slavery. But how far would he go? A white, militant antislavery reformer named John Brown had a violent plan he wanted Douglass to be part of. It might even include murder.

8

My Friend, the President

One of Douglass's frequent guests at his Rochester home was John Brown. Douglass and Brown shared the same ideas about the evils of slavery. They often wrote to each other. In the mid-1850s, Brown was a guerrilla fighter battling proslavery advocates in Kansas. The U.S. government had decided that the people of Kansas should choose for themselves whether to be a slave or free state. The result was almost a civil war between proslavery and antislavery forces in a state that became known as "Bleeding Kansas."

Brown left Kansas to work on a massive slave revolt. He planned to steal weapons from a federal arsenal in the town of Harpers Ferry, Virginia (today Harpers Ferry, West Virginia). He would launch an attack on the arsenal. With the weapons, he would capture slave owners around Harpers Ferry and hold them hostage. He and his volunteers would give the weapons to the slaves. The armed slaves would then revolt against their owners.

Brown invited Douglass to meet with him and a handful of supporters in Chambersburg, Pennsylvania. There Brown told Douglass his idea. Douglass thought it was crazy. First, attacking a federal arsenal is a serious crime. It would not win friends for Douglass and the abolitionist movement.

Second, Douglass did not think it was well thought out. After Brown explained it, Douglass recalled, "I looked at him with some astonishment . . . and told him that Virginia would blow him and his hostages sky high, rather than that he should hold Harper's Ferry [sic] an hour."[1]

Brown Follows Through

Douglass went back to Rochester, and Brown went ahead with his plans. On October 16, 1859, Brown and his band of supporters seized the arsenal at Harpers Ferry. Soon, federal troops led by Colonel Robert E. Lee surrounded Brown and his men. Brown was captured and accused of treason. Two months later, a court found Brown guilty and he was hanged.

Douglass felt he had done nothing wrong because he had rejected any part in Brown's scheme. Yet people discovered letters Brown and Douglass wrote to each other. Those seemed to make Douglass guilty by association. Douglass knew he would never get a fair trial if he was brought to the slaveholding state of Virginia. The only thing he felt he could do to be safe was leave the country. He hopped aboard a boat and sailed to Canada.

Douglass had previously made plans to give a series of lectures in London in late 1859 into 1860. From the safety of Canada, he boarded an England-bound ship in November 1859. Douglass arrived in the port city of Liverpool, England, on November 24. He was as popular as ever in England. However, his speaking tour was cut short when he was in Glasgow, Scotland. There, he received word that his little daughter Annie had died on March 13, 1860. Douglass was heartbroken. Despite the danger of arrest, he knew he had to return home.

Douglass was lucky. Since the Harpers Ferry incident was such an emotional issue, the government decided not to pursue it any further after Brown had been hanged. They thought it was best if the country moved beyond it. Douglass went back to work, lecturing and working on a new publication: *Douglass's Monthly.*

The Strange Election of 1860

One of the nation's most unusual election campaigns in history took place in 1860. The Democratic Party split into the Northern and Southern Democrats. There were also several independent parties. One, the Constitutional Union Party, was strongly antislavery. They nominated Douglass's friend Gerrit Smith as their candidate. However, Douglass felt Smith could not win. Douglass supported Abraham Lincoln from the Republican Party.

Shortly after Lincoln won the election in November, South Carolina seceded from the Union. They believed Lincoln would put an end to slavery. Slavery was the basis of the Southern economy, which relied heavily on agriculture. In the weeks that followed, ten more slave-holding states seceded in rapid succession. They formed their own nation: the Confederate States of America, also known as the Confederacy. On April 12, 1861, Confederate forces attacked federal Fort Sumter off the coast of Charleston, South Carolina. The Civil War was underway.

During the early months of the war, Lincoln stressed that his goal was to preserve the Union. He said he would not interfere in states where slavery remained legal. But Douglass urged Lincoln to abolish slavery. Douglass also insisted that the Union should allow African Americans to enlist in the Army. The Army at the time was all white.

In the September 1861 issue of *Douglass's Monthly,* Douglass wrote an essay titled, "Fighting Rebels With Only One Hand." In it Douglass asked, "Why does the Government reject the Negro? Is he not a man? Can he not wield a sword, fire a gun, march and countermarch, and obey orders like any other?"[2]

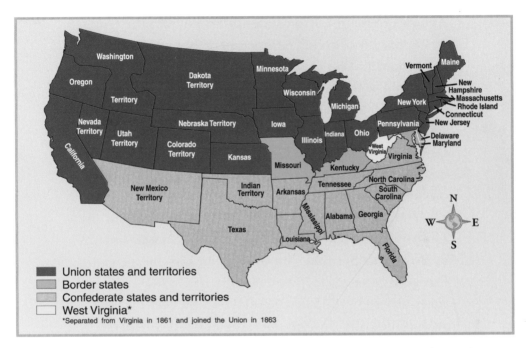

A map of the United States at the time of the Civil War shows the Union and Confederate states and territories. The border states remained part of the Union; many of them still had slavery. West Virginia broke away from Confederate Virginia in 1861 to become its own state in the Union.

The North expected to win the war with ease. It had more soldiers and more resources. But early on, the Northern generals bumbled while the South hung tough. Near the end of 1862, the North was not close to winning. Lincoln felt something drastic needed to be done.

The First Emancipation Proclamation

On September 22, 1862, Lincoln issued a document that ordered all slaves of the Confederate States of

America to be free if the states did not rejoin the Union by January 1, 1863. The document became known as the Emancipation Proclamation. The proclamation did not apply in the four border states: Missouri, Kentucky, Maryland, and Delaware. Those were slaveholding states that had not seceded. Lincoln feared that freeing slaves in the border states would cause them to rebel and secede. The Emancipation Proclamation took effect on January 1, 1863.

Douglass and his supporters were thrilled by Lincoln's New Year's Day announcement.[3] Douglass was in Boston at the time. Word reached him by telegram. Douglass later said, "The effect of this announcement was startling beyond description, and the scene was wild and grand. Joy and gladness exhausted all forms of expression from shouts of praise, to sobs and tears."[4]

The Right to Fight

Douglass reached one of his goals in 1863 when Congress passed a law allowing African Americans to serve in the Union army. Douglass actively recruited young African-American men from upstate New York. He was proud to say that the first man to sign up was his son Charles. His son Lewis enlisted as well. Douglass himself was forty-four years old. That made him a bit old for an active soldier's job.

Recruiting black men was not easy, especially when they learned that black soldiers were paid less than white soldiers. The Army also did not permit them to advance in rank beyond noncommissioned officers.

In addition, the Confederate Congress passed a law in 1863 stating that captured African Americans would be treated as rebel slaves, which would likely mean a death sentence.

Douglass objected and said he would stop recruiting African Americans until the U.S. government did something in response to the Confederacy's new law. President Lincoln took note. On July 30, 1863, he signed an order stating that "for every soldier of the United States killed in violation of the laws of war a rebel soldier shall be executed."[5] The laws of war that Lincoln referred to included: limiting the war to achieving the diplomatic goals that started the war; protecting civilians; and ending the war as quickly as possible.

The next month, Douglass met with Samuel C. Pomeroy, an abolitionist senator from Kansas. Douglass expressed his concerns about discrimination against African Americans in the military. Pomeroy took Douglass to meet Secretary of War Edwin M. Stanton. Douglass found Stanton rude and inconsiderate. So Douglass met with another abolitionist friend to arrange a meeting with the president himself.

Meeting With Mr. Lincoln

Douglass and Lincoln met in the White House on August 10, 1863. Douglass first thanked Lincoln for signing the July 30 order. Douglass then brought up the subject of poor treatment and unfair pay for African-American soldiers. Lincoln said he would do what he could to make pay and treatment more equal.

The Massachusetts 54th Regiment

The Massachusetts 54th Regiment became the first all African-American unit in the Union Army. Colonel Robert Gould Shaw, a white man, commanded the unit during the war.

The Massachusetts 54th had its biggest challenge in the summer of 1863. On July 18, it led an attack on Fort Wagner, located on Morris Island off the South Carolina coast. The 54th bombarded the fort, then charged it. The fighting was filled with fierce hand-to-hand combat, but the Confederates held their ground. The Massachusetts 54th suffered high casualties. Colonel Shaw and 281 members of the 54th were killed.[6] The survivors retreated. Yet the battle was a moral victory, since it proved the bravery and strength of African-American soldiers.

Douglass's son Lewis wrote two days after the battle, "This regiment has established its reputation as a fighting regiment. Not a man flinched, though it was a trying time. I have been in two fights and am unhurt. . . . Men fell all around me. How I got out of that fight alive I cannot tell."[7]

However, he implied that such advances must be made in small steps. That answer did not fully satisfy Douglass. But he assured Lincoln he would continue his recruiting efforts.

The next year was a presidential election year. With the war going poorly for the North, it seemed likely that Lincoln would not be reelected. One group called the Radical Republicans thought Lincoln moved too slowly on the abolition issue. They split from the

President Abraham Lincoln

Republican Party (called the National Union Party during the 1864 election), forming the Radical Republican Party and nominated John C. Fremont as their presidential candidate. At first, Douglass supported Fremont for president.

Douglass met with Lincoln a second time on August 19, 1864. Douglass recalled that Lincoln was depressed about the war. Even though the North had won some major battles such as Gettysburg a year earlier, the president still worried that the North might lose. Douglass asked Lincoln to plan to lead slaves out of the South if the North was defeated. Lincoln told Douglass he was working on such a plan. Lincoln did not give Douglass any specific information on how this would be done. Still, Douglass left the meeting with faith in the president.[8]

The Massachusetts 54th Regiment stormed Fort Wagner, proving their bravery in battle. The all African-American unit suffered heavy casualties during the battle.

A few things happened over the next several weeks to change Douglass's mind about supporting Fremont. Union generals William Tecumseh Sherman and Philip Sheridan won major victories in the South. Around the same time, Union admiral David G. Farragut captured Mobile Bay in Alabama. The war was turning in favor of the Union.

The Democrats selected General George B. McClellan as their nominee. There were fears among Douglass and other abolitionists that if the people elected McClellan he would compromise with the South. That might include canceling Lincoln's Emancipation Proclamation, allowing Southerners to keep their slaves.

Lincoln's the One

Douglass was concerned that with the split caused by the Radical Republican Party, McClellan might be elected president. With that in mind, he switched his support to Lincoln.

With the North making military progress, Fremont dropped out of the race. He and the other Radical Republicans also threw their support to Lincoln. Lincoln chose the governor of Tennessee, Andrew Johnson, as his running mate. Johnson was from the opposition Democratic Party. But unlike most southern Democrats, Johnson was part of a group of Democrats, called the "War Democrats," that supported the Union.

Lincoln and Johnson won in a landslide. Douglass wrote with satisfaction: "His election silenced, in a good degree, the discontent felt at the length of the war, and the complaints of it being an Abolition war."[9]

Lincoln was officially inaugurated for his second term as president on March 4, 1865. That evening, Douglass and an African-American friend, Sarah Dorsey, planned to join the many Americans greeting Lincoln in the White House. With the spirit of Lincoln's address in mind, Douglass expected that he would be welcome. Douglass wrote:

> . . . though no colored [African-American] persons had ever ventured to present themselves on such occasions, it seemed now that freedom had become the law of the republic, now that colored men were on the battle-field mingling their blood

with that of white men in one common effort to save the country, it was not too great an assumption for a colored man to offer his congratulations to the President with those of other citizens.[10]

But to many whites, the idea of a black man greeting the president at such a notable event was outrageous. As soon as Douglass and Dorsey reached the White House door, two policemen grabbed Douglass's arm and pulled him aside. They had been given orders not to allow any African Americans into the White House. The officers led Douglass and Dorsey through the White House in the direction of an exit.

At that moment, a White House staff member recognized Douglass. He told the staff member to tell Lincoln that he was being held against his will. Word was sent to Lincoln who called for Douglass to come and greet him.

Lincoln Welcomes His Friend

As soon as Lincoln saw Douglass, the president exclaimed, "Here comes my friend Douglass."[11] Lincoln said it loudly enough that those around him could easily hear. In the eyes of the president of the United States, Frederick Douglass was not just a guest. He was the president's *friend*.

Lincoln asked Douglass what he thought of his speech. Douglass asked Lincoln if he really wanted to hear his opinion since thousands of other people were waiting to shake Lincoln's hand. Lincoln replied that he strongly valued Douglass's opinion. Douglass complimented the president on his address, and Lincoln thanked him for his opinion.

Demanding the Vote

Although Douglass was satisfied with Lincoln's reelection, he did not back down on his views, even if they seemed radical at the time. In early April 1865, Douglass gave a speech titled, "What the Black Man Wants." In it, Douglass demanded the right to vote. He said:

> *I have had but one idea for the last three years, to present to the American people, and the phraseology in which I clothe it is the old abolition phraseology. I am for the 'immediate, unconditional, and universal' enfranchisement of the black man, in every State in the Union. Without this, his liberty is a mockery; without this, you might as well almost retain the old name of slavery for his condition; for, in fact, if he is not the slave of the individual master, he is the slave of society, and holds his liberty as a privilege, not as a right.*[12]

A few days later, on April 14, 1865, John Wilkes Booth assassinated President Lincoln. Douglass heard the news at home. In shock, the citizens of Rochester made their way to city hall. A few people, including Douglass, gave speeches. Douglass later wrote, "We shared in common a terrible calamity, and this 'touch of nature, made us' more than countrymen, it made us 'kin.'"[13]

The Lion of Anacostia

O n December 6, 1865, the Thirteenth Amendment to the U.S. Constitution was ratified. The amendment outlawed slavery in the entire United States.

Finally, Douglass achieved his lifetime goal. He considered retiring from active life. But African Americans begged him not to. The Southern states lay in poverty and ruin. It would take years for the South to be rebuilt. The region began a period called Reconstruction.

In the meantime, many southerners treated African Americans as poorly as they had been when they were slaves. African Americans had difficulty finding work in the South. Those who were unemployed in some states were arrested and fined. Those who could not pay the fines were placed into forced labor—basically the same as slavery.

An Official Post for Douglass

Douglass realized he was needed. He went back to work and took on the cause of African-American suffrage. He met with Lincoln's successor, President Andrew Johnson. Johnson was not ready to go so far as to advocate for African-American voting rights. However, he did offer Douglass an inviting position: head of the Freedmen's Bureau. The federal government had established the Freedmen's Bureau after the war. Its purpose was to provide food, clothing, shelter, education, and jobs to newly freed slaves. Douglass was tempted to take the position. But by doing so, it might seem to African Americans that he was supporting Johnson's policies. Douglass did not want to give that impression and rejected the offer.

Civil War hero General Ulysses S. Grant received the Republican nomination for president in 1868, and Douglass campaigned vigorously for him. Douglass and other African Americans believed that with Grant as president there was a good chance that the Constitution would be amended to grant African Americans the right to vote. Grant won an overwhelming victory over Democrat Horatio Seymour.

A Rift With Woman Suffragists

While Douglass pushed for African-American suffrage, he did not do the same for the voting rights of women. As a result, his friendships with feminists Elizabeth Cady Stanton and Susan B. Anthony soured.

Douglass spoke to a group of woman suffragists in May 1869. Speaking on behalf of oppressed African Americans, Douglass tried to justify his viewpoint. He said:

> *With us, the matter is a question of life and death, at least, in fifteen States of the Union [sic]. When women, because they are women, are hunted down through . . . New York and New Orleans; when they are dragged from their houses and hung upon lampposts; when their children are torn from their arms, and their brains dashed out upon the pavement; when they are objects of insult and outrage at every turn; when they are in danger of having their homes burnt down over their heads; when their children are not allowed to enter schools; then they will have an urgency to obtain the ballot equal to our own.* [1]

A woman in the audience questioned Douglass whether that was also true of African-American women.

Douglass responded, "Yes, yes, yes; it is true of the black woman, but not because she is a woman, but because she is black."[2]

While Douglass was upsetting woman suffragists, they in turn were making African Americans just as angry. Stanton and Anthony accepted money from a wealthy Democrat named George Train who supported votes for women. But Train was very prejudiced against African Americans. He hoped that when white women could vote, they would help pass laws hostile to African Americans.[3] Stanton and Anthony justified their actions by saying it was up to women to do whatever they could to gain suffrage. To them, that meant getting donations, from whomever the source may be, to continue fighting for their cause.

Frederick Douglass fell out of favor with suffragists like Elizabeth Cady Stanton when he supported the Fifteenth Amendment, which did not call for woman suffrage.

African Americans had something to celebrate on March 30, 1870. On that day, the Fifteenth Amendment to the Constitution was ratified. It states that no citizen of the United States, regardless of race, color, or previous condition of servitude, or life as a slave, should be denied the right to vote. Since gender was not mentioned in the amendment, states still had the right to deny women the right to vote.

Grant.   Dulany. Duglass Revels.   Colfax.

PUBLISHED & PRINTED BY   Entered according to act of Congress in the year 1870 by Th. Kelly in the Office of the Librarian of Congress at Washington D.C.   THOMAS KELLY 17 BARCLAY ST N.Y.

THE FIFTEENTH AMENDMENT

1 Reading Emancipation Proclamation
2 Life Liberty and Independence
3 We Unite the Bonds of Fellowship
4 Our Charter of Rights the Holy Scriptures

5 Education will prove the Equality the Races
6 Liberty Protects the Marriage Alter
7 Celebration of Fifteenth Amendment May 19th 1870
8 The Ballot Box is open to us.

9 Our representive Sits in the National Legislature
10 The Holy Ordinances or Religion are free
11 Freedom unites the Family Circle
12 We will protect our Country as it defends our Rights.

13 We till our own Fields.
14 The Right of Citizens of the U.S. to vote shall not
be denied or abridged by the U.S. or any State on account
of Race Color or Condition of Servitude 15th Amendmt

This poster celebrates the ratification of the Fifteenth Amendment. Frederick Douglass is shown at the top of the poster, flanked by two other prominent African Americans—Martin Robinson Delany, an author and the first black major in the U.S. Army, to the left, and Mississippi senator Hiram Rhoades Revels.

A Strange Inferno

On a June night in 1872, Douglass was in Washington when he received a telegram stating that his Rochester house had been almost totally destroyed by fire. The good news was that Douglass's family was safe.

Douglass was convinced that the fire was caused by arson, or set on purpose.[4] He decided to leave Rochester and move to Washington, D.C. Historians have offered different reasons why. Some say Douglass was convinced the fire was set by racists, and that made Rochester unsafe in his mind. Others say he merely wanted to be in the heart of the nation's political hub.

Regardless, the family settled in Washington. Frederick Douglass immediately went to work campaigning for the reelection of President Grant in 1872. In November, Grant won in a landslide.

Frederick Douglass: Bank President

Douglass returned to the lecture circuit. In 1874, the Freedman's Savings and Trust Company, a national bank, gave him a special opportunity. It had been founded in 1865 as a special place for freed slaves to invest their money. The bank's trustees, people elected to make decisions on how the bank should be run, asked Douglass if he would be president of the bank.

There was one problem. The bank was losing money. Banks then were not insured by law as they are today. Douglass took the job and worked hard to save the bank. But Douglass was a writer and lecturer, not a banker. The bank went out of business. It was a public embarrassment for Douglass.[5] It also hurt Douglass in another way. He lost twelve thousand dollars he had invested in the bank.

Frederick Douglass: Marshal

Douglass began to lecture again. That was one way to earn back much of the money he had lost. The next

U.S. president, Rutherford B. Hayes, named Douglass marshal of the District of Columbia. Douglass's job was to oversee the criminal justice system in Washington, D.C. However, he had a large staff working under him. Douglass's duties were mainly ceremonial.[6]

Hayes had become president as a result of a very close election. A lot of deal-making had taken place. In order to win votes from southern states, Hayes said he would end Reconstruction in the South. That meant that the federal government would remove its troops from the former Confederate states. Since these federal troops were key to protecting freed slaves, much of the African-American community was angry at Hayes. Some were also angry at Douglass for taking a position offered by Hayes.

Being awarded a government office was a milestone for an African American, however. Furthermore, the job allowed Douglass to stay in Washington with his family. He took advantage of the position to move into a new home in the Anacostia section of Washington. The stately home, which still stands today, is called Cedar Hill. It has white columns outside and fourteen rooms.

It also includes a large library with room for Douglass's collection of two thousand books.[7] Douglass decorated the library walls with portraits of people who meant a lot to him. These included those he had rifts with, including William Lloyd Garrison and Susan B. Anthony. The house had a sprawling backyard, which gave his grandchildren plenty of room to romp and play. Douglass, now viewed as a seasoned veteran of the battle to end slavery, became known as The Lion of Anacostia.

Frederick Douglass's house, Cedar Hill, is a national historic site today.

A Meeting With His Former Owner

In June 1877, Douglass took a little trip that was sure to bring back memories. He returned to his boyhood home in St. Michaels, Maryland. Douglass walked into a brick house that was home to Thomas Auld, his owner so many decades ago. Auld was now a dying man. He and Douglass spoke for about twenty minutes.

Douglass asked about his family members. Auld corrected Douglass by saying he did not send Douglass's grandmother Betsey Bailey into the woods to die. Douglass had written that accusation in his famed "Letter to His Old Master." Instead, Auld had brought her to St. Michaels to be cared for until her death. Douglass apologized for his false statement.[8]

Douglass asked about his birth date. Although Douglass thought he was born in 1817, Auld insisted it was 1818. At one point, Douglass asked Auld what he had thought about his escape.

Auld replied, "Frederick, I always knew you were too smart to be a slave, and had I been in your place I should have done as you did."[9]

Douglass answered, "Capt. Auld, I am glad to hear you say this. I did not run away from *you*, but from *slavery.*"[10]

Was Douglass Too Forgiving?

Some African Americans were disappointed that Douglass visited his former owner. To them, Douglass was far too forgiving of a man who had enslaved him. Douglass wrote in response: "I had no business with this man under the old regime but to keep out of his way. But now that slavery was destroyed, and the slave and the master stood upon equal ground, I was not only willing to meet him, but was very glad to do so."[11]

Douglass continued his duties as marshal until the next president, James A. Garfield, took office in 1881. Garfield gave the job of marshal to a personal friend. He appointed Douglass the recorder of deeds for Washington, D.C. Douglass headed the office that recorded property sales in the city. It was a step down for Douglass. Still, he humbled himself and took the post. Though the job may not have been Douglass's

In 1881, a Philadelphia publisher created this poster that featured Frederick Douglass (center). To Douglass's left is Blanche Kelso Bruce, a former senator and President James A. Garfield's register of the Treasury and to Douglass's right is Hiram Rhoades Revels, a former senator from Mississippi.

first choice, it did give him spare time to write. It was in 1881 that Douglass finished his third autobiography, titled, *The Life and Times of Frederick Douglass.* The book brought readers up to date in his life—from his childhood through the Civil War years to his work in Washington.

Anna's Death

Douglass's good times came to a sudden stop on August 4, 1882. Douglass's wife, Anna, died of a stroke.

The couple had been married for forty-four years. Douglass fell into a severe depression and did not feel like doing anything.[12] To try to improve his mood, he saw a doctor. The doctor said Douglass needed total rest. Some friends took Douglass to the resort town of Poland Springs, Maine. In time, Douglass felt well enough to return to Washington to go back to work.

One clerk who worked under Douglass was Helen Pitts, a white woman in her mid-forties. Despite the race and age differences, Pitts and Douglass had a lot in common. They shared similar political views. They both played musical instruments; he played violin, and she played piano. The two got along together so well that they married on January 24, 1884.

In 1884, interracial marriage was shocking. The headline in one newspaper read:

A Black Man's Bride

Frederick Douglass Married Last Night
to Miss Helen Pitts.

The Woman Young, Attractive, Intelligent,
and White.[13]

Many members of Helen's family now refused to have anything to do with her. That was despite the fact that they were abolitionists. Even Douglass's own children were upset.[14] African-American activists found Douglass's marriage an insult to African-American women.

Honeymoon in Niagara Falls

Frederick and Helen Douglass ignored their critics. They took a honeymoon to Niagara Falls. Then they spent much of 1886 and 1887 traveling through Europe and Africa. In the election year 1888, Douglass campaigned for Republican Benjamin Harrison. After winning the presidency, Harrison appointed Douglass to his biggest post yet: minister and consul general to the mostly black Caribbean nation of Haiti. Today, Douglass's title would be ambassador. An ambassador is a nation's official representative to another nation. Howard University professor Thomas Battle said, "Putting [Douglass] out there as a representative of America, I think, was in a sense a crowning point of his career."[15]

In 1892, Chicago hosted a world's fair, which had exhibits about the world's countries. The 1892 world's fair was officially titled the World's Columbian Exposition. Douglass was appointed commissioner of Haiti's exhibit. His job was to supervise the exhibit's construction and design.

Douglass planned for the exhibit to showcase the achievements of the Haitian people. Yet exhibits in other parts of the world's fair portrayed native Africans as primitive and uncivilized. It was the exact opposite of the message Douglass tried to send about Hatians, who were the descendants of Africans.

On February 20, 1895, Douglas went to a meeting of the National Council of Women attended by Susan B. Anthony. She and Douglass had overcome their differences. That day she greeted him and led him to

Frederick Douglass and his wife, Helen (left), pose for a picture with Helen's sister, Eva Pitts.

the rostrum where he would speak. After his speech, Douglass returned home to Cedar Hill. That evening he suffered a massive heart attack. Shortly afterward, Frederick Douglass died.

Douglass's funeral took place four days later. Senators and other dignitaries attended, and all the schools for African-American children in Washington were closed to honor the fallen leader. He was buried in Mount Hope Cemetery in Rochester, New York, next to the bodies of his wife Anna and daughter Annie.

Legacy

t is interesting to think of the life Frederick Douglass would have lived had he been born one hundred years later. He certainly would have been involved in the civil rights movement. But would he have stressed nonviolence like Dr. Martin Luther King, Jr.? Or would he have adopted a more militant political stance like Malcolm X's "By any means necessary?"

Perhaps he would have taken the middle ground. Like Dr. King, Douglass mostly believed in nonviolent resistance. However, there were times when he felt violence might be necessary to end slavery. That was especially true in the 1850s when the Civil War was on the horizon. Yet even after his primary goal— the abolition of slavery—was reached, Douglass continued the struggle for equality for all.

Frederick Douglass is buried in Mount Hope Cemetery in Rochester, New York.

Historian Frank Faragasso writes, "In the long struggle for freedom and equality for all people Douglass was a vital figure. He began as an abolitionist concerned with the freeing of the slaves. . . . He also reminded us that freedom and equality are never freely granted but must be gained through struggle and agitation."[1]

Another historian, Vincent Harding, summed up Douglass's continuing appeal more than a century after his death. Harding says, "Douglass hoped that America might be the place that he could give witness to as a great nation. He saw its possibilities. He saw its potentials. And he was willing to struggle for the nation to become a great nation with black people making powerful contributions to the building of that kind of nation."[2]

CHRONOLOGY

1818 — Born Frederick Augustus Washington Bailey in February at Holmes Hill Farm, near Easton, Maryland.

1824 — Taken from grandmother and moves to Wye House to begin life as slave; witnesses first slave beating.

1826 — Moves to Baltimore to live with Hugh and Sophia Auld.

1827 — Sophia Auld helps teach Frederick to read.

ca.
1831 — Buys first copy of *The Columbian Orator.*

1833 — Sent to live with Thomas and Rowena Auld in St. Michaels, Maryland.

1834 — Sent to live with slave breaker Edward Covey, who beats Frederick often; Frederick attempts to run away but is returned; holds his own in fight with Covey.

1835 — Sent to live on farm owned by William Freeland.

1836 — Attempts escape on April 2 but is caught and sent to jail; moves back to live with Hugh Auld family.

1837 — Founds East Baltimore Mental Improvement Society.

1838 — Successfully escapes on September 3; marries Anna Murray; settles in New Bedford, Massachusetts; changes name, first to Frederick Johnson, then to Frederick Douglass.

1839 — First subscribes to *The Liberator*; gives first public speech in a church on March 12; daughter Rosetta born on June 24.

1840 — Son Lewis Henry born on October 9.

1841 — First public speech to a formal audience in Nantucket, Massachusetts; hired as public speaker by William Lloyd Garrison; moves to Lynn, Massachusetts.

1842 — Son Frederick, Jr., born on March 3.

1843 — Beaten by anti-abolitionist mob in Pendleton, Indiana, on September 16.

1844 — Son Charles Remond born on October 21.

1845 — First autobiography published; begins tour of British Isles.

1846 — Ellen Richardson and friends help Douglass officially buy his freedom from Thomas Auld.

1847 — Returns to United States; moves to Rochester, New York; first edition of his newspaper *The North Star* published on December 3.

1848 — Takes part in first women's rights convention in Seneca Falls, New York; "Letter to His Old Master" published in *The North Star.*

1849 — Daughter Rosetta not allowed to attend public school in Rochester; daughter Annie born on March 22.

1851 — Changes name of *The North Star* to *Frederick Douglass' Paper.*

1852 — Gives speech, "What to the Slave Is the Fourth of July?" on July 5.

1855 — Second autobiography is published.

1859 — Rejects joining slave rebellion plot led by John Brown; escapes to Canada; travels to England for speaking tour.

1860—Daughter Annie dies; Douglass returns home from England.

1863—Lincoln announces Emancipation Proclamation on January 1; Douglass meets with Lincoln on August 10.

1864—Meets Lincoln for a second time on August 19.

1865—Lincoln assassinated on April 14; Thirteenth Amendment to the Constitution abolishing slavery ratified on December 6.

1870—Fifteenth Amendment to the Constitution ratified on March 30, giving the right to vote to male African Americans.

1872—Home in Rochester burns; Douglasses relocate to Washington, D.C.

1874—Named president of Freedman's Saving and Trust Company, but bank fails.

1877—Named marshal of Washington, D.C.; returns to boyhood home to visit old slave owner.

1881—Named recorder of deeds in Washington, D.C.; publishes third and last autobiography.

1882—Wife, Anna, dies on August 4; Douglass falls into deep depression.

1884—Marries Helen Pitts, a white woman, causing major controversy.

1886–1887—Travels with wife to Europe and Africa.

1889—Appointed minister and consul general to Haiti.

1892—Commissioner for Haiti exhibit at World's Columbia Exposition in Chicago.

1895—Dies on February 20.

CHAPTER NOTES

CHAPTER 1
Escape!

1. Benjamin Quarles, ed., *Great Lives Observed: Frederick Douglass* (Englewood Cliffs, N.J.: Prentice-Hall, Inc., 1968), p. 31.
2. Dickson J. Preston, *Young Frederick Douglass* (Baltimore: The Johns Hopkins University Press, 1980), pp. 155–156.
3. Quarles, p. 32.

CHAPTER 2
When Reading Was a Crime

1. Personal e-mail from Chief Historian Frank Faragasso, Frederick Douglass National Historic Site, Washington, D.C., June 4, 2008.
2. George DeWan, "Slavery Died a Slow Death," *Newsday* Web site, November 15, 2007, © 2008, <http://www.newsday.com/community/guide/lihistory/ny-history-hs 511a,0,6240189.story> (August 4, 2008).
3. Craig Haffner and Donna E. Lusitana executive producers, "Frederick Douglass," *Biography* series, Greystone Communications, Inc., in association with A&E Networks, copyright 1994 Hearts/ABC/NBC.
4. William S. McFeely, *Frederick Douglass* (New York: W. W. Norton & Company, 1991), p. 13; Sandra Thomas, *"Frederick Douglass: Abolitionist/Editor,"* "The Slave Years," n.d., <http://www.history.rochester.edu/class/douglass/part1.html> (October 1, 2006).
5. Frederick Douglass, *Narrative of My Life* (New York: Literary Classics of the United States, 1994, originally written 1845), p. 16.
6. Ibid.

7. Tamara E. Robinson executive producer, "Frederick Douglass: When the Lion Wrote History," copyright 1994, Greater Washington Educational Telecommunications, Inc.
8. Douglass, p. 19.
9. Ibid.
10. Frederick Douglass, *My Bondage and My Freedom* (New York: Literary Classics of the United States, 1994, originally written 1855), p. 157.
11. McFeely, p. 27.
12. Ibid., p. 30.
13. Douglass, *My Bondage and My Freedom*, p. 224.
14. Frederick Douglass, *The Life and Times of Frederick Douglass* (New York: Citadel Press, 1995, originally published in 1881), p. 74.
15. Robinson, "Frederick Douglass: When the Lion Wrote History."
16. Waldo E. Martin, Jr., *The Mind of Frederick Douglass* (Chapel Hill, N.C.: The University of North Carolina Press, 1984), p. 8.
17. "The Inflation Calculator" Web site, creator and maintainer: S. Morgan Friedman, based on Consumer Price Index statistics from *Historical Statistics of the United States* (USPGO, 1975), <www.westegg.com/inflation> (November 21, 2007).
18. "The Influence of *The Columbian Orator*," Assumption College Web site, n.d., <http://www.assumption.edu/ahc/rhetoric/columbianoratorfront.gif> (January 30, 2008).

CHAPTER 3
Breaking the Slave Breaker

1. Frederick Douglass, *My Bondage and My Freedom* (New York: Literary Classics of the United States, 1994, originally published in 1855), p. 250.
2. Waldo E. Martin, Jr., *The Mind of Frederick Douglass* (Chapel Hill, N.C.: The University of North Carolina Press, 1984), p. 10.
3. Douglass, p. 251.
4. William S. McFeely, *Frederick Douglass* (New York: W. W. Norton & Company, 1991), p. 44.
5. Martin, p. 12.

6. Dickson J. Preston, *Young Frederick Douglass*, (Baltimore: The Johns Hopkins University Press, 1980), p.125.
7. Frederick Douglass, *Narrative of the Life of Frederick Douglass: An American Slave*, (New Haven: Yale University Press, 2001), p. 53.
8. Ibid., p. 54.
9. Ibid.
10. Preston, p. 130.
11. Douglass, *Narrative of the Life of Frederick Douglass: An American Slave*, p. 60.
12. Douglass, *My Bondage and My Freedom*, p. 324.

CHAPTER 4
The Lure of Freedom

1. Frederick Douglass, *The Life and Times of Frederick Douglass* (New York: Citadel Press, 1995, originally published in 1881), p. 170.
2. Ibid., p. 171.
3. Dickson J. Preston, *Young Frederick Douglass* (Baltimore: The Johns Hopkins University Press, 1980), p.140.
4. Ibid.
5. Ibid., p. 142.
6. "The Inflation Calculator" Web site, creator and maintainer: S. Morgan Friedman, based on Consumer Price Index statistics from *Historical Statistics of the United States* (USPGO, 1975), <http://www.westegg.com/inflation/infl.cgi> (December 20, 2007).
7. Douglass, p. 191.

CHAPTER 5
A New Life in New Bedford

1. Frederick Douglass, *The Life and Times of Frederick Douglass* (New York: Citadel Press, 1995, originally published in 1881), p. 202.
2. Ibid.
3. William S. McFeely, *Frederick Douglass* (New York: W. W. Norton & Company, 1991), p. 72.

4. Frederick Douglass, *Narrative of the Life of Frederick Douglass: An American Slave,* (New Haven: Yale University Press, 2001), p. 77.
5. Personal e-mail from Chief Historian Frank Faragasso, Frederick Douglass National Historic Site, Washington, D.C., June 4, 2008.
6. Ibid.
7. "The Inflation Calculator" Web site, creator and maintainer: S. Morgan Friedman, based on Consumer Price Index statistics from *Historical Statistics of the United States* (USPGO, 1975), <www.westegg.com/inflation> (January 11, 2008).
8. Sandra Thomas, *"Frederick Douglass: Abolitionist/Editor,"* "From Slave to Abolitionist/Editor," n.d., <http://www.history.rochester.edu/class/douglass/part2.html> (October 1, 2006).
9. James Oakes, *The Radical and the Republican* (New York: W. W. Norton & Company, 2007), p. 111.
10. Thomas.
11. Douglass, *The Life and Times of Frederick Douglass*, pp. 214–215.
12. Ibid., p. 215.
13. Charles Waddell Chesnutt, *Frederick Douglass: A Biography* (ebooksread.com, February 8, 2004, release date, originally published 1899), <http://www.ebooksread.com/authors-eng/charles-waddell-chesnutt/frederick-douglass-689/1-frederick-douglass-689.shtml> (January 11, 2008).
14. Ibid.
15. Ibid.

CHAPTER 6
"As a Speaker, He Has Few Equals"

1. Sandra Thomas, *"Frederick Douglass: Abolitionist/Editor,"* "From Slave to Abolitionist/Editor," n.d., <http://www.history.rochester.edu/class/douglass/part2.html> (October 1, 2006).
2. Ibid.
3. Waldo E. Martin, Jr., *The Mind of Frederick Douglass* (Chapel Hill, N.C.: The University of North Carolina Press, 1984), p. 25.

4. Benjamin Soskis, "Heroic Exile: The Transatlantic Development of Frederick Douglass 1845–1847," n.d., <http://www.yale.edu/glc/soskis/fr-5.htm> (January 18, 2008).
5. Frederick Douglass, [Letter], Glasgow (Scotland), April 16, 1846. To William Lloyd Garrison, from *The Liberator*, 15 May 1846; Reprinted in Philip Foner, ed., *Life and Writings of Frederick Douglass*, vol. 1 (New York: International Publishers, 1950), p. 149, republished at "Documenting the American South,"n.d.,<http://docsouth.unc.edu/neh/douglass/support11.html> (November 7, 2007).
6. Frederick Douglass, originally published in the Sheffield *Mercury*, September 12, 1846, republished at "Documenting the American South," n.d., <http://docsouth.unc.edu/neh/douglass/support5.html> (November 7, 2007).
7. Thomas.
8. Soskis.
9. The Inflation Calculator" Web site, creator and maintainer: S. Morgan Friedman, based on Consumer Price Index statistics from *Historical Statistics of the United States* (USPGO, 1975), <www.westegg.com/inflation> (January 21, 2008).
10. Personal e-mail from Chief Historian Frank Faragasso, Frederick Douglass National Historic Site, Washington, D.C., June 4, 2008.

CHAPTER 7
His Own North Star

1. William S. McFeely, *Frederick Douglass* (New York: W. W. Norton & Company, 1991), p. 149.
2. The Library of Congress Web site, "American Treasures of the Library of Congress," November 21, 2002, <http://www.loc.gov/exhibits/treasures/trr085.html> (January 23, 2008).
3. The Library of Congress Web site, n.d.,<http://www.americaslibrary.gov/aa/douglass/aa_douglass_leader_1_e.html> (January 23, 2008).
4. Personal e-mail from Chief Historian Frank Faragasso, Frederick Douglass National Historic Site, Washington, D.C., June 4, 2008.

5. Phone interview with Anne Derousie, Historian, Women's Rights National Historical Park, May 15, 2008.
6. Frederick Douglass, *My Bondage and My Freedom* (Making of America Books digital library), n.d., <http://quod.lib.umich.edu/cgi/t/text/pageviewer-idx?c=moa;cc=moa;idno=abt6496.0001.001;frm=frameset;view=text;seq=428;page=root;size=s> (January 24, 2008).
7. Douglass, <http://quod.lib.umich.edu/cgi/t/text/pageviewer-idx?c=moa;cc=moa;idno=abt6496.0001.001;frm=frameset;view=text;seq=430;page=root;size=s>
8. Waldo E. Martin, Jr., *The Mind of Frederick Douglass* (Chapel Hill, N.C.: The University of North Carolina Press, 1984), p. 25.
9. Lara Crigger, "Local History: Rochester's Lost Underground Railroad," *Rochester City Newspaper*, originally published September 26, 2007, <http://www.rochestercitynewspaper.com/news/articles/LOCAL+HISTORY:+Rochester+s+lost+Underground+Railroad/> (January 24, 2008).
10. "The Meaning of July Fourth for the Negro," *Africans in America* series, PBS Web site, 1950, <http://www.pbs.org/wgbh/aia/part4/4h2927t.html> (November 10, 2007).
11. Tamara E. Robinson executive producer, "Frederick Douglass: When the Lion Wrote History," copyright 1994, Greater Washington Educational Telecommunications, Inc.

CHAPTER 8
My Friend, the President

1. Frederick Douglass, *The Life and Times of Frederick Douglass* (New York: Citadel Press, 1995, originally published in 1881), p. 324.
2. "Three Speeches from Frederick Douglass: Examples of his Passion, Logic and Power," from *The Life and Writings of Frederick Douglass*, (Five volumes) by Philip S. Foner, International Publishers. Fremarjo Enterprises, Inc., © 1997, <http://www.frederickdouglass.org/speeches/index.html#wants> (January 26, 2008).
3. Douglass, p. 359.
4. Ibid.
5. William S. McFeely, *Frederick Douglass* (New York: W. W. Norton & Company, 1991), p. 228.

6. Elaine Louie, "Chronicle," *The New York Times* Web site, September 17, 1997, <http://query.nytimes.com/gst/full page.html?res=9E02EFDB1538F934A2575AC0A961958 260> (May 14, 2008).

7. Craig Haffner and Donna E. Lusitana, executive producers, "Frederick Douglass," Biography series, Greystone Communications, Inc., in association with A&E Networks, copyright 1994 Hearts/ABC/NBC.

8. Sandra Thomas, *"Frederick Douglass: Abolitionist/Editor,"* "From Slave to Abolitionist/Editor," n.d., <http://www .history.rochester.edu/class/douglass/part2.html> (October 1, 2006).

9. Douglass, p. 368.

10. Ibid., p. 371.

11. Thomas.

12. "University of Rochester Frederick Douglass Project," n.d., <http://www.library.rochester.edu/index.cfm?PAGE= 2946> (November 18, 2007).

13. Douglass, p. 379.

CHAPTER 9
The Lion of Anacostia

1. Waldo E. Martin, Jr., *The Mind of Frederick Douglass* (Chapel Hill, N.C.: The University of North Carolina Press, 1984), p. 159.

2. Ibid.

3. *"All Men and Women Are Created Equal: The Story of Women's Rights National Historical Park, Seneca Falls, New York"* (Published by Eastern National, 2005), p. 61.

4. Ibid.

5. William S. McFeely, *Frederick Douglass* (New York: W. W. Norton & Company, 1991), pp. 285–286.

6. Sandra Thomas, *"Life After the 13th Amendment,"* "From Slave to Abolitionist/Editor," n.d., <http://www.history. rochester.edu/class/douglass/part5.html> (October 1, 2006).

7. James Oakes, *The Radical and the Republican* (New York: W. W. Norton & Company, 2007), p. 276.

8. Frederick Douglass, *My Bondage and My Freedom* (New York: Literary Classics of the United States, 1994, originally published in 1855), p. 877.

9. Frederick Douglass, *The Life and Times of Frederick Douglass* (New York: Citadel Press, 1995, originally published in 1881), p. 448.
10. Ibid.
11. Ibid., pp. 446–447.
12. McFeely, p. 313.
13. Craig Haffner and Donna E. Lusitana executive producers, "Frederick Douglass," *Biography* series, Greystone Communications, Inc., in association with A&E Networks, copyright 1994 Hearts/ABC/NBC.
14. Martin, p. 99.
15. Haffner and Lusitana.

CHAPTER 10
Legacy

1. Personal e-mail from Chief Historian Frank Faragasso, Frederick Douglass National Historic Site, Washington, D.C., June 4, 2008.
2. Tamara E. Robinson, executive producer, "Frederick Douglass: When the Lion Wrote History," copyright 1994, Greater Washington Educational Telecommunications, Inc.

GLOSSARY

abolitionism—The belief that slavery should be abolished or stopped.

African Methodist Episcopal (AME) Church—A denomination of Christianity that broke away from the United Methodist Church and is followed mainly by African Americans.

border states—The four slaveholding states that did not join the Confederacy during the Civil War: Delaware, Maryland, Kentucky, and Missouri.

caulker—A person who fills seams on a ship with a waterproof substance, making the boat water-tight.

colonization movement—A controversial belief that slavery in the United States should be ended by relocating American slaves and other African Americans back to Africa.

consul general—A government employee who represents his or her home nation to another nation and resides in that foreign nation.

emancipation—Freedom from slavery.

Freedmen's Bureau—A government department started after the end of the Civil War to provide food, clothing, education, and other necessities to newly freed slaves.

Reconstruction—The period after the Civil War (from 1865–1877) when the former Confederate states were ruled by the Union.

secede—To officially withdraw from a group, organization, or nation.

slave breaker—A person who tried to turn rebellious slaves into productive laborers, usually through force.

suffrage—The right to vote.

Underground Railroad—The informal name for a network of places where escaped slaves were allowed to stay while heading to freedom.

FURTHER READING

Burchard, Peter. *Frederick Douglass: For the Great Family of Man.* New York: Simon & Schuster Children's Publishing, 2003.

Collier, James Lincoln. *The Frederick Douglass You Never Knew.* Danbury, Conn.: Children's Press, 2004.

Mayer, Cassie. *Frederick Douglass.* Portsmouth, N.H.: Heinemann, 2007.

Ruffin, Frances E. *Frederick Douglass: Rising Up from Slavery.* New York: Sterling Publishing, 2008.

Ruggiero, Adriane. *American Voices from Reconstruction.* New York: Marshall Cavendish Benchmark, 2007.

Uschan, Michael V. *Reconstruction.* Farmington Hills, Mich.: Gale Group, 2007.

Internet Addresses

The Frederick Douglass papers
at the Library of Congress
<http://memory.loc.gov/ammem/doughtml/doughome.html>

Frederick Douglass National Historic Site
<http://www.nps.gov/frdo>
Frederick Douglass's Washington, D.C. home, Cedar Hill

Mr. Lincoln's White House: Frederick Douglass
<http://www.mrlincolnswhitehouse.org/inside.asp?ID=38&subjectID=2>

INDEX

10/09